65 SUCCESSFUL HARVARD BUSINESS SCHOOL APPLICATION ESSAYS

SECOND EDITION

With Analysis by the Staff of *The Harbus*, the Harvard Business School Newspaper

ST. MARTIN'S GRIFFIN  NEW YORK

65 SUCCESSFUL HARVARD BUSINESS SCHOOL APPLICATION ESSAYS, SECOND EDITION.
 Printed in the United States of America. For information, address St. Martin's Press, 175 Fifth Avenue, New York, N.Y. 10010.

www.stmartins.com

Library of Congress Cataloging-in-Publication Data

65 successful Harvard Business School application essays : with analysis by the staff of *The Harbus*, the Harvard Business School newspaper / Lauren Sullivan and the staff of *The Harbus*.—2nd ed.

p. cm.

ISBN 978-0-312-55007-3

1. Business schools—United States—Admission. 2. Exposition (Rhetoric) 3. Essay—Authorship. 4. Business writing. 5. Harvard Business School. I. Sullivan, Lauren. II. *Harbus*. III. Title: Sixty-five successful Harvard Business School application essays.

HF1131.A135 2009

808'.06665—dc22

2009012531

First Edition: August 2009

10 9 8 7 6 5 4 3 2 1

CONTENTS

Contents

III. Career Aspirations

IV. Typical Day

V. Three accomplishments

Contents

Contents

ACKNOWLEDGMENTS

The motivation to create the second edition of *65 Successful Harvard Business School Application Essays* came from a recent rise in business school applications. With an abundance of qualified candidates to choose from, admissions officers can be more selective, making admission to top schools even more challenging for applicants. *The Harbus*, the Harvard Business School weekly student newspaper, recognizes that applicants require up-to-date materials and inspiration to match the current environment. While this book includes the latest application essays, which are updated regularly by the admissions committee, it retains several essays from the first edition of the book because of their uniqueness as well as to reflect typical question topics that may reappear in future admissions' applications.

It is worth noting that this book is created by The Harbus News Corporation, an independent nonprofit entity, not the Harvard Business School. The Harbus contributes profits to a grant-making foundation that supports community organizations and schools in the Boston area. The Foundation to date has awarded over $850,000 in grants to forty organizations that pursue initiatives in education and literacy.

The views and opinions expressed in this book do not necessarily reflect those of Harvard Business School, and the references to the school throughout the book do not mean that the school endorses these views or opinions.

Acknowledgments

A huge credit is owed to five contributors from the Class of 2008 and Class of 2009 who helped source the content, select essays, and write critiques and chapter introductions: Aastha Gurbax and Uma Subramanian from the Class of 2008 and Will Boland, Linda Dempah, and Zachary Surak from the Class of 2009. We thank all the HBS students and alumni who kindly shared their personal essays. We would also like to thank the staff of the Harbus, including Lauren Sullivan, Marianne Bakula, and Christie Cuthbert, for their encouragement and support. Lastly, we would be remiss if we did not express our gratitude for assistance from our agent, Katie Boyle, and our editor at St. Martin's, Matthew Martz.

INTRODUCTION

You are inspired, hopeful, accomplished, and eager. You seek personal and professional advancement via an MBA that will prepare you for leadership challenges in any business field. You are aware, however, that Harvard Business School receives about ten thousand applications annually, and you are uncertain how to make your application stand out. We understand. We have been in your shoes.

This book seeks to demystify the admissions process for applicants by providing a selective but robust sample of HBS essays that have successfully survived the admissions committee in the past. We aspire to show you a variety of writing styles, essay responses, and applicant backgrounds that have been successful in the past, but there are no foolproof prescriptions, shorts cuts, or magic formulas. There are probably as many perfect application essays as there are applicants.

The chosen essays highlight ordinary applicants who have demonstrated potential, vision, integrity, and leadership. While the MBA applicant pool can often swarm with people with business backgrounds, we are positive that this book will also inspire nontraditional applicants because they will realize that there is no such thing as a standard applicant at Harvard Business School. We encourage you to bear in mind that your profession is not what makes the essay special. What makes you special is how you make the big (or small) decisions in life and how they have led to your growth. The only common strain in the successful essays is that applicants have clearly described why each experience is challenging, educational, and transformational. We hope this book motivates you to write great essays by revealing who you really are. Be captivating. Be truthful. Be yourself.

When you sit down at a blank computer screen, you may be tempted to think that your experiences to date have been rather pedestrian. You are neither an Olympic gold medalist nor a Pulitzer Prize winner. We hope that the examples in this book will rescue you from this fear. Many of the essays contain simple anecdotes with routine settings that demonstrate the applicant's maturity, awareness, and potential. Use anecdotes from *your* life to offer an astute glimpse into your personality, sense of humor, values, thoughtfulness, and all other attributes that will contribute to your success in life and business. Even the most prestigious accomplishment will be deficient if you do not explain why it was important, what you learned from it, and how you have grown because of it.

First, make a mental list of the most influential and meaningful events and experiences of your life and begin to map them into your essays, but avoid repetition. While you may want to weave a few overarching themes in all your essays, use the essays to demonstrate different aspects of your intellectual, emotional, and moral fiber. For instance, if you choose to prove your ability as a competent project manager in one essay, you may wish to discuss a more personal issue like your relationship with your parents or partner in the next. Reach inside yourself for examples of strength, confidence, and accomplishment.

In the end, your fundamental objective is to prove that you are greater than the sum of your individual application parts such as your GMAT score, academic transcripts, or professional laurels. While those parts of the application are significant, your essays will allow you to bring your charisma and individuality to life. So, steer clear of cut-and-paste jobs from the resume.

Once you map out the essays, you will find the word limit excruciating. Although an obstacle, the word count can help you tell your story more selectively and succinctly. After all, does your employer want you to be unnecessarily long-winded and unfocused? Probably not. The essays included in this book will convince you that you can be poignant in few words. We suggest that you create the first draft without a strict word limit. In the subsequent draft, ask yourself repeatedly: "What is my core message? Does this sentence improve upon or clarify that message?" By doing this, you will be able to distill the key anecdotes and interpretations from a pool of excessive descriptions and unnecessary details.

The essays in this book will help you to assess and celebrate your key experiences in a robust fashion. In the analyses, we consider each author's motivations, accomplishments, and shortcomings and assess whether they communicate them compellingly and credibly through their choices of content, structure, and style. We have selected essays that deliver the author's message in a way that stood out from the pack—your ultimate goal as an applicant. To do the same, concentrate on the frank analysis that follows each essay. The constructive suggestions, embedded in the analyses, will enable you to avoid common pitfalls and convert a good set of application essays into a remarkable one.

We believe that you will find the sixty-five essays that follow to be useful examples, but remember to treat them only as examples. Let your uniqueness shine through your own essays and not through imitation of the essays in this book. We cannot promise you that this book will get you into Harvard Business School. There are books, Web sites, and admission consultants that promise such things, falsely. We do not. With this book, however, you will have the tools to get the job done and truly own your business career, so good luck!

Aastha Gurbax

Publisher, Harbus News Corporation, Class of 2008

On behalf of Harbus News Corporation

I. DEFINING MOMENT

Discuss a defining experience in your leadership development. How did this experience highlight your strengths and weaknesses as a leader?

This question may appear quite daunting. By default many applicants first think about their most significant accomplishments. If you have led troops in battle or started a nonprofit, you may think you have this essay in the bag. That is the first trap of this subtle question. A "defining experience" is not necessarily one that results in achievement relative to peers. In fact, some of the strongest essays focus on monumental failures. Sometimes focusing on a failure actually allows you to answer the question more easily. Many people fail to reflect on their weaknesses and to delve deeply enough into the lessons they have learned. I assure you, you do not have to be Superman to get into business school. Reveal a little of your Clark Kent side. In doing so, you will not only address each component of the essay topic but you will also, and more importantly, become a more interesting applicant.

There is no particular calculus behind what type of anecdote to pick. Just dig deep. Be introspective. Find an anecdote that describes what makes you unique as a person and a leader. Find that story that talks about how you developed into who you are today. Then tell that story with passion. Explain both your actions and thought processes. Leave the reader with a deep understanding of your motivations, character, and goals.

If you choose to focus on an accomplishment, this essay can be a great opportunity for you to add color to something that does not jump off your resume. Though while adding color, make sure you leaven it with humility. Arrogance is one trait that the admissions staff will not appreciate.

—Zachary Surak

Stacie Hogya

A great leader aspires to do more than simply accomplish her objective. Until I offered to lead a team of skeptical engineers and accountants to develop a marketing department, and to actively participate in business development, I did not recognize how valuable the "more" could be.

I began the project at a disadvantage; the owners had already spent three months and $20,000 with an advertising agency, but developed no usable material. I wanted to inspire my team's confidence as I led them into the unknown world of marketing, so I took several strong, decisive actions. I fired the agency and hired a more contemporary group whose personality was a closer match to what my firm wanted to broadcast. I established a marketing committee and presented them with a vivid vision of our goals and my plan to achieve them. While confidence-inspiring, these decisive actions had an undesired consequence: I discouraged my team from providing their input. My actions indicated that I had already made all of the decisions, and that the team's suggestions would carry no weight.

I had to change my leadership approach to focus on facilitating collaboration rather than dictating a course of action. Because our consultants present information in a systematic and analytical fashion when communicating with our clients, I took this familiar approach in my communications with my team. Instead of presenting my strategy and looking for feedback, I coached the team through the process, and we developed strategies together.

As a result, the consulting team took ownership of the project and got more involved. We worked with the new agency to create an identity that highlighted our unique personality. Marketing committee meetings were well-attended, and members were active participants; they planned business development initiatives under the theme, "Growing the business is everybody's business." Most importantly, many of the consulting team members personally thanked me for making participation in business development so easy.

Through this experience, I matured as a leader and learned that leading is as much about accomplishing your objective as it is about holding your team together. I learned the value of guiding my team to define a shared vision in which we could all be stakeholders rather than simply presenting a strategy. I was most effective by leading strongly enough to inspire confidence but not so strongly that I prevented involvement.

ANALYSIS

Stacie's experience may look very similar to your experience. Do not fret. Her essay is traditional in both its anecdote and style. Many applicants will discuss lessons learned when effecting change from a consultative role. More still will start their essay with a thesis statement, followed by an example, and end with more detailed reflection on the example. That being said, Stacie still manages to stand out in several ways.

When competing with thousands of essays on the same topic,

grabbing the reader's attention with a compelling opening paragraph can be a key differentiator. Beginning with a personal statement on leadership and a brief description of the management challenge Stacie faced stimulates the reader's curiosity about the context and resolution.

Throughout the rest of the essay, Stacie reinforces the outcomes of her actions with strong logic. Despite her initial failure, she establishes herself as an effective leader who takes time to analyze the situation, reflects on her actions and mistakes, devises a tactical plan, and leads her team to achieve their desired outcome. Stacie exhibits strong self-awareness and a willingness to recognize her mistakes and leaves no doubt as to her ability to build consensus and lead change.

What makes this essay come together is Stacie's nuanced, mature takeaway in the final paragraph: effective leadership is not as black and white as choosing whether to articulate a vision or coach others. There is a healthy balance that effective leaders must continually manage. In her conclusions about what traits contribute to management success, Stacie demonstrates her potential for leadership in business. Future applicants should strive to do the same.

ANONYMOUS

R. J. O'Leary, a retired Marine and three-war veteran who mentored my father, presented the offer: "Son, how 'bout I find you a real job next summer." Fifteen years old, I had just completed two mind-numbing months of employment at a burger shack. I didn't wait for an explanation; I accepted.

The Padlock Ranch stretches from the snow-capped Big Horn Mountains in Wyoming to the short-grass prairie of southern Montana. I arrived and joined the Forks crew: twelve men, fifty-six horses, and three thousand cattle. On my first day, the foreman, Tony, sat at the head of the dinner table. I walked in and he announced, "Here's our cowboy from Rhode Island." The room fell deathly silent.

It was branding season. I took the bruising job of wrestling calves. After branding season, I joined the fencing crew, five men led by the oldest hand, Morris. We worked ten-hour days planting railroad ties and anchoring fence braces. I admired Morris's expertise and calm demeanor. But Morris never did any physical work, and he constantly aired his disdain for fencing.

After two weeks, Morris abruptly quit. Tony approached me. He said that I had earned his trust and wanted me to lead the crew. I replied that I would be honored but first wanted to consult Lon, now the oldest crew member (twice my age). Lon, a quiet man, was not interested in taking on more responsibility. I told Lon I respected him and asked for his support. "You've got it," he replied.

Our team struggled at first. I remained focused and took on the unglamorous jobs, such as pounding the rocky soil to set fence posts into the ground. I spoke for the team and represented all members favorably to Tony, even when some performed poorly. This promoted loyalty within our group. I went to Lon for advice. Not only did he offer useful feedback, but he became more invested in the team. After two weeks, our performance improved. Soon, each member of the team pushed the others to work harder. This was my first true glimpse at leadership. It inspired me. Just like at the Forks, I now lead small teams of men who are older, more experienced, and generally more technically proficient than I am. The Forks taught me to take chances, lead from the front, promote a team mentality and loyalty, and work with the strongest members to improve the weakest.

ANALYSIS

Despite using atypical elements like quotes, this essay comes across as incredibly thoughtful and well-organized with enough originality to make the applicant memorable. The essay exudes maturity. The author discusses a challenge that many young professionals face—trying to lead a group with members who possess more experience than the leader. Rather than use his own voice to describe the situation at the Padlock Ranch, the author brings in voices from three different characters in the story. His unique form of narrative effectively uses these voices to drive home key points and takeaways that might come across less powerfully if he paraphrased them. His use of quotes also saves him space in a word-constrained essay, allowing him to redeploy his words to describe the situation more deeply and emphasize his conclusion. Even though the conclusion is relatively brief in its explicit discussion of takeaways, the author coyly embeds his lessons learned throughout in places like Morris's leadership strengths and interactions with Lon.

The author also comes across as a very humble and insightful leader. He provides evidence that he is willing to take direction from the people he is leading and "represent all team members favorably" to the boss. These traits will translate well to a business school environment where as much learning occurs on a peer-to-peer basis outside the classroom as from professors in the classroom.

Most importantly, the author directly connects this decade-old ranching experience to his current job where he leads "older, more experienced, and generally more technically proficient" employees. In doing so, he clearly demonstrates how this experience has had a meaningful impact on how he chooses to lead. Be sure to remember that what you've learned from the experience is much more important than the experience itself.

ANONYMOUS

In my senior year of college, I was selected from a pool of more than fifty applicants to serve as one of ten student directors for the Big Siblings Program. Shortly into my tenure, school guidance counselors reported that a number of volunteers had failed to establish contact with their little siblings. Refusing to accept this unfortunate but recurring problem, I resolved to change it. My initial reaction was to launch a supplemental recruiting effort to replace the inactive volunteers. The other directors, however, believed that a concerted attempt to engage dormant volunteers would be more effective. To that end, we contacted our inactive volunteers to understand their circumstances and discovered that many lacked ideas to engage their little siblings or felt uncomfortable interacting outside the university community.

In response to these concerns, I developed a plan to organize and advertise various on-campus group social activities. I excitedly outlined the project's various benefits and offered to coordinate the group's efforts, thereby overcoming the directors' initial skepticism regarding the time commitment required. I organized the directors into pairs to brainstorm and implement one unique group activity, creating personal ownership in the project and an open forum for exchanging ideas. Recognizing that a compelling example could drive the plan forward, I took the initiative to plan the first event. Despite my personal embarrassment of donning a full Santa suit, the inaugural Holiday Party was successful, attracting more than fifty volunteers. Furthermore, three events implemented by the directors later that year resulted in 75 percent of the inactive volunteers ultimately contacting their little siblings. I was extremely proud that our efforts had enhanced the program's impact, and I felt for the first time that I had meaningfully connected with my community.

This experience helped me realize that my drive to implement solutions quickly can cause me to overlook certain details when analyzing problems. Had I replaced inactive volunteers based on my original assumption that they were lazy and unconcerned, I would have missed the opportunity to devise the plan that jump-started their involvement. This experience also highlighted leadership strengths that balance this weakness. Most important, I am a good listener. Openness to others' input allows me a broader perspective for analyzing problems and leads to more thorough solutions. Furthermore, I pour my heart into everything I do. My enthusiasm enables me to work well in teams, motivate others, and create a fun and supportive team environment.

ANALYSIS

This essay is evidence that the right choice of anecdote will set you up for success. The author chooses a situation with a clearly defined problem, and then points to measurable impact as a direct result of his actions. The reader is left having to connect very few dots, ensuring that the author's intended message gets conveyed. The more unconnected dots in your essay, the more room there is for the reader to arrive at the wrong or at least a less powerful conclusion.

This essay's greatest strength, however, lies in the author's subtle framing of his strengths and his weaknesses. He clearly answers that part of the question by pointing to a bias for action as something that would have made him arrive at a less "thorough" solution. But does this weakness sound like a deep-seated character flaw? No. In fact, many readers can probably point to circumstances where this trait could be perceived as a strength. Consider this outcome a strategic victory for the author. He leaves the audience believing his weakness will actually help him lead on occasion. Framing the weakness in this way helps mitigate this essay's greatest cause of angst: leaving oneself defenseless against criticism. It is human nature to cringe at the thought of having to discuss our mistakes and flaws (which may be why some people fail to even answer that part of the prompt), but don't run away from the challenge. Tackle it head-on, but like this author, be selective in your choice of topic. Do not use the essay to confess your greatest professional sins (that might preclude you from getting into business school), but rather use it as an opportunity to show how you have grown.

David La Fiura

I dreaded Mondays during the winter of 2004–2005. I dealt with problems: we ran into the wrong silo, ruining 150,000 pounds of material (a $75,000 mistake), Line 4's motor blew, and the 1600 jammed. We just moved to the seven-day schedule, which meant running sixty hours without management on-site. I *hated* Mondays.

As the new production manager at Ultra-Poly's main plant, I managed the company's largest department through the biggest expansion of its thirty-year history. That fall we doubled capacity by transitioning to a twenty-four-hour, seven-day schedule and installing a fifth production line. The department's workforce grew from thirty to sixty-five-plus in two months.

My first challenge was devising a strategy to facilitate the schedule change. Initially employees, unhappy with prospects of working twelve-hour shifts, threatened to quit. I realized employees' anger stemmed from their perceived powerlessness. My proposal, designed to win support for change through communication and employee involvement, included interviewing every employee. In meetings, I explained the company's need for change and presented scheduling options. Importantly, employees determined the adopted schedule via companywide vote. Thus, they controlled part of the process that fostered support. I built consensus and, amazingly, no employees left after the change.

Despite higher capacity, output dropped after we started running seven days. Restructuring meant experienced employees were spread thin. Mistakes caused downtime and quality problems. As pressure mounted, increasing production became critical. We needed to train the thirty-plus new employees fast. I initiated and oversaw development of an extruder-operator training course, complete with custom videos, tests, and certification criteria. The program delivered results: since early 2005, fifteen operators have been certified and daily production has increased by 25 percent.

Facilitating change highlighted my strong communication skills and grasp of organizational theory. Leading through the ensuing adversity required vision and confidence. At times however, my lack of management experience caused problems. Accurately setting expectations was difficult initially, and learning was a process of trial and error: low expectations meant underperformance, but unreasonably high expectations caused confusion and animosity. My solution was to gain expertise in the process. Understanding the equipment's capabilities provided an important guide for setting expectations. Though I still need experience, I understand the value of the perspective it provides. Since the transition, the workforce has solidified and production exceeds forecasts. Successfully leading the department through this dramatic growth stage was the most challenging and rewarding experience of my career.

ANALYSIS

From the outset, David establishes a very human connection with the reader. How many of us, after all, have felt some anxiety about returning to work at the beginning of the week? He draws us in further with his detailed description of the troubles he encounters, seemingly pulling the reader onto the plant floor alongside him with vivid imagery.

Beyond this compelling introduction, much of this essay's strength lies in its organization. Notice how naturally and cogently the story progresses. David quickly moves from setting the stage in the first two paragraphs, to defining a problem, describing his role in crafting a solution, and discussing the outcome. Throughout, the focus remains on the results—"no employees left after the change." He adds further depth, complexity, and credibility to his story by discussing some unintended consequences of his actions as well as the efforts he led to mitigate them, again focusing on the tangible results of his leadership.

The essay's only faults lie in David's last paragraph where he addresses the second part of the essay prompt: *How did this experience highlight your strengths and weaknesses as a leader?* His lack of managerial experience does not differentiate him from the rest of the young managers and analysts in the applicant pool where such failings are common. That's a given. The pitfall is that the essay allows an admissions officer to wonder why David needs business school instead of more work experience. Applicants should not shy away from using a real weakness (i.e., not a disguised strength or a simple lack of experience), and use it as an opportunity to show their honesty, self-awareness, and their personal development as a leader.

Second, the essay clearly demonstrates how his strengths and experiences as a leader will make him a strong contributor to the school community, but in leading the project, he applied leadership skills he had already learned, e.g., consensus-building and communicating a vision. Writing about a reinforcing moment rather than a defining moment doesn't make for a flawed essay. These moments can very clearly get their points across as David's essay did, but they normally have less impact because the change isn't striking or significant.

ANONYMOUS

During a course field visit to Benin, I toured a hospital where doctors substituted plastic baggies for sterile latex gloves. Patients had no hospital gowns, sheets, or mattresses. Supply shortages resulted in the reuse of needles. Before leaving, I made a promise to doctors and villagers to help improve their health conditions. To fulfill this pledge, I cofounded a 501(c)3 nonprofit organization, Project Bokonon, which addresses acute medical conditions in Benin and spreads awareness of West African poverty in the United States.

To insure its sustainability, I designed an institutional infrastructure and composed bylaws. I recruited young professionals and students to a nineteen-member board of directors and organized a kickoff event to formally introduce the organization to the community. Raising over $25,000, cultivating donors, and recruiting volunteers, I visited over fifteen schools and universities and thirty conferences and civic organizations. On one educational visit, I traveled to a Harlem middle school. Though I worried that the audience, some of the poorest children in America, might not understand why we were sending resources elsewhere, the question-and-answer session concluded with a student asking, "How can *we* help?" This same young boy waited until the auditorium cleared to open his wallet and to hand me a lone dollar. His request: "Please spend this for me in Africa."

My experience managing the inaugural board illuminated my

lack of experience. I depended too heavily on e-mail correspondence and learned when a phone call or face-to-face meeting might be a more appropriate medium. I further assumed everyone shared equal levels of commitment. I also underestimated the difficulty of managing the expectations of those whom we intended to serve. Nevertheless, I learned about a leadership style I strive to adopt: servant leadership, which focuses on leading by serving first.

While good organizational skills and strategic thinking might make a good manager, effective servant leaders help others not only identify how they can contribute to a process but also inspire their hearts to connect an idea to action. My Project Bokonon experience defined for me the significance of enabling others, like the Harlem student, to act. In only a few years, Project Bokonon has built a clinic, established formal partnerships with other nonprofits and the United States Peace Corps, and serves ten health sites because of the lesson learned in the utility of sharing the ownership of a promise with others.

ANALYSIS

The author is not your average applicant. Not everyone at business school has founded a nonprofit organization. For those that have, or have experiences that are not directly tied to traditional business school professions, this is an opportunity to stand out. It is important to note, however, that leadership comes in many different forms and does not require a grandiose project or setting. Merely starting a nonprofit does not explain what makes this a defining experience in one's leadership development. A successful applicant needs to diligently answer the question at hand while telling a story that provides insight into the applicant's life, character, and goals. The author's accomplishment certainly stands on its own, but she also directly answers the question in the context of this exceptional life experience. She shares that she deeply values empowering others to act but recognizes that sometimes, to her detriment, she overestimates others' commitment to their shared vision. She understands that she must adapt her style to her context to connect the hearts and minds of those she leads. Through this color, the reader develops a well-rounded picture of the author's personality, beyond simply her accomplishments, as well as her personal definition of leadership as service—another point that sets her apart from the broader applicant pool.

That being said, the author could have improved her essay by shedding more light on her emotional reaction to the conditions in Benin. An unfiltered statement like, "I found the conditions appalling" would have given the reader even more context to understand her actions. Similarly, she could have gone into more detail regarding her motivations for such drastic action. Starting a not-for-profit is not necessarily the most obvious answer to the problems she discovered.

The author not only has the substance that makes her memorable, she also tells the story in a manner that resonates. The imagery and voice of the young boy from Harlem who asked that his dollar be spent in Africa is indelibly etched on the reader's memory long after completing the essay. These essays are opportunities to voice a message, and this author clearly captures the hearts and minds of her readers.

Avin Bansal

This past summer, the VP and the only other associate on my team left Summit. The associate, my mentor, had been instrumental in helping me build financial and sales abilities in sourcing new opportunities. Without his and the VP's support, I knew that I would be called upon to "step up" and that my leadership would be tested in new and unforeseen ways. This quickly proved to be true when two new associates joined Summit, bringing little work experience and needing significant mentoring.

Thrust into mentoring, I have moved quickly to help the new associates stretch beyond their defined roles, spending countless hours teaching them the technical and interpersonal aspects of our positions. Through both organized and impromptu training sessions, I coach them on sales pitches, industry dynamics, algorithms for quick company evaluation, and financial modeling. Additionally, I advise them on balancing work and personal life, a skill rarely discussed in private equity. Interestingly, mentoring has sharpened my own skills. My understanding of leadership is no longer about getting people "to do or follow"; rather, it is about expanding intellect to release untapped resources, vision, and action. The results corroborate this belief; these new associates have quickly become as productive as more experienced Summit associates.

While becoming the "voice of experience" for the new associates, I have also become a more independent and therefore more useful asset to my superiors. I have embraced the concept of leadership in terms of guidance, using my in-depth evaluation of companies to guide my VP and principal to deals of exceptional quality. Recently, I found a $25 million information services company eager to arrange an investment quickly. Rather than remaining in the background, I again stepped up, joining my new VP in meeting and evaluating the company in person, a rare practice among associates. Today, we are at the brink of a $36 million investment in the company. By assuming some of my superiors' responsibilities, I have simultaneously lessened their burden and enhanced my own leadership.

When my teammates left Summit, I felt a little abandoned. Though I never doubted my ability to master the leadership challenge I faced, I am delighted to have discovered that I can be both creative and methodical in my quest to lead people and organizations. By consistently focusing on my self-improvement while finding ways to extract teammates' untapped value, I can be a leader without directly managing people or holding a special title.

ANALYSIS

Many applicants with only a few years of work experience probably identify with Avin's situation. In fact, informal leadership opportunities in a financial service firm may be one of the most common themes among essays reflecting on leadership experiences. Avin's employer, Summit, seems typical of companies in the sector where mentorship occurs informally and individual effectiveness is measured in terms of investment returns. Nevertheless, Avin points out that even in these caldrons of seemingly inert leadership, there are always opportunities for individuals to develop into team players and mentors.

Without formal authority, Avin is "thrust" into a leadership position when his firm hires new associates. He quickly learns that mentoring is more than getting people "to do or follow." So far so good, in terms of explaining his defining moment. But Avin stumbles in trying to state a succinct thesis. The poignant takeaway we are expecting is muddled by business-ese. What exactly does it mean to "expand intellect to release untapped resources"? Avin could have done a better job of editing here by simplifying his leadership thesis to something like, "Leadership is about getting people to perform better than they ever anticipated they could."

Luckily for Avin, his message still comes across vis-à-vis a pair of targeted, brief examples. We understand how he impacted the productivity of the inexperienced associates, while also improving his own ability to develop business opportunities. Indeed, his examples leave very little room for incorrect interpretation or extrapolation. Furthermore, at the end of the day, Avin leaves nothing to chance. In the essay's final sentence, he ensures that his readers will understand his point by restating his thesis, this time much more clearly. While some essays repeat takeaways unnecessarily, Avin's conclusion works here by tying together his two very different examples. This type of conclusion often works well when discussing multiple examples in one essay.

Anonymous

As the London Shine Project champion during 2003/04, I taught English and Math to students in disadvantaged schools. The program director approached me to help students with behavioral difficulties.

Meeting these children compelled me to get involved even though I lacked formal training. At the age of ten, these students had been caught in the destructive web of smashing windows, shoplifting, bullying younger students, and constantly underperforming academically.

Instead of a PwC partner or a potential client, my key target had transformed into an international student who knew twenty words in English, mostly obscenities. This was a defining moment for me as I felt unprepared as a leader. "How can I help a child whose opening greeting to me is an obscenity?" I thought.

I requested enrollment in a course for dealing with difficult kids. The course, though useful, could not prepare me for the upcoming obstacles. I created a flexible plan to account for students' unpredictable reactions. I had to be empathetic and effective while remaining within the scope of U.K. child protection laws.

A friendly get-together with ice cream served as an icebreaker. I carried out further sessions in the congenial setting of the school park. I encouraged students to discuss what made them happy. The answers ranged from "spending time with my granddad" to "beating up students." I chose to listen without being judgmental. The students slowly opened up after I shared my life experiences. I was able to earn their trust by being honest yet fun.

In group sessions, we used anecdotes to discuss the accepted values of society. We practiced simple anger management techniques like counting from one to ten. I channeled their energies in creative and harmless pursuits such as oil painting and drawing facial expressions to express feelings. While these sessions helped me in understanding them, they helped the children in managing their aggression.

When the student who specialized in breaking windows gave me his beautiful oil painting, I understood that my time and energy had been well spent. After a year of mentoring, three of the four students are now calmer, kinder, and perform in the top 10 percent of their class. Personally, I progressed as a leader by addressing my weakness of impatience. This experience taught me that as an agent of change, one does not necessarily need corporate experience; instead, one requires creativity, patience, and emotional intelligence.

ANALYSIS

The writer of this essay creates a study of contrast in her defining leadership experience. While the applicant clearly has significant corporate experience, the encounter with "difficult kids" shows how the writer overcame adversity in an unfamiliar environment. The strength of the essay lies in the deliberate attention to detail surrounding the levers that motivated the children to change. In explaining the steps to reform underperforming students, the applicant clearly conveys her logic, not requiring the reader to connect the dots alone. The high level of detail and the honest description of the emotions she experienced add credibility to the story. Furthermore, the author leaves the impression that she is a strong teacher, mentor, and problem-solver, admirable qualities in a leader.

This essay would have been stronger if the applicant had spent less time describing the situation and more time developing her takeaways. While the logic to the applicant's actions and positive outcome are abundantly clear, the author slights herself by dedicating only the two final sentences to the lessons she learned from this experience. While her takeaway is clear, logical, and profound, more of the essay is about the journey of self-discovery than the discovery itself. Try not to fall into a similar trap. If you find yourself at a loss for words, reflect on how the lessons have impacted subsequent endeavors. Talk about how you may still be working to overcome your weakness. Just make sure that the discovery—your concluding thought to the reader—does not underwhelm following an otherwise strong essay.

Brad Finkbeiner

I didn't know what to believe, and with hypothermia setting in, I didn't know if I could make it. The water was 48°F and I had been in it for thirty minutes. Luckily, I was headed back to shore, but it had been a frustrating experience. I had always been a good swimmer and I could have made it back before now, but those weren't the rules. The twelve of us were instructed to swim and finish as a team. Then again, the same people told us the water would be warm and to jump in without wet suits. After another twenty minutes and constant encouragement, we finally made it. My feeling of pride and newfound confidence showed me just how much I had needed the challenge.

Eagle Lake Wilderness Camp in the Colorado Rockies provided fourteen days of cold, hunger, and exhaustion, which turned into a lifetime of opportunities. Growing up, I was smart and perceptive, but also reserved. I needed to break that paradigm. I needed confidence in my ability to handle stressful, unpredictable situations so that I could develop my potential as a leader.

Our swim was only one of ten challenges faced by our team. I learned much more than how to survive hypothermia, navigate a free rappel, live in and off the wilderness, and complete a high-altitude half-marathon. I revealed some of my natural leadership qualities like self-understanding and sustained motivation. I demonstrated how to work effectively within teams. I acquired the confidence to pursue leadership responsibilities. I found the will to pursue difficult and exhausting goals along with the stamina to accomplish them. And I learned how to be most effective by encouraging and developing others.

Our team mantra, "This wasn't in the brochure," has since reflected the excitement and challenge of my life. Without the lessons and confidence gained from this experience, I would never have had the ability to run student governments, organize community initiatives, or lead consulting project teams.

ANALYSIS

The outdoors-experience-that-changed-my-life story runs the risk of sounding all too familiar but does not in this case, thanks to Brad's nice sense of storytelling. Brad goes into the experience as a shy kid without a lot of confidence but emerges from the hypothermia, the half-marathon, and the free rappel as a more courageous and confident person. The transformation is striking, and Brad proves that he is someone open to new experiences. Brad does a nice job with this essay by describing in detail both how he changed and what he learned from the experiences. When writing your own essay, if you are worried your topic might not come across as super-original, take the time to tell a compelling narrative with lots of colorful details. The more specific you are, the better your essay will be.

Brad concludes his essay by mentioning his participation in student government, community work, and leadership at work. These are great illustrations of the impact of his "defining experience." While he lacks room in this essay to elaborate on them, if used thematically throughout the rest of his essays, these common threads could give the reader a coherent, mutually supporting picture of the applicant. Furthermore, while Brad does an effective job highlighting his leadership strengths, he could have improved his essay meaningfully if he had discussed how this experience highlighted his leadership weaknesses as well. The most important leadership lessons are often found in your setbacks or mistakes, and reflecting on these will show the admissions committee that you possess strong self-awareness and a willingness to learn and adapt.

Anonymous

In November 2004, violent anti-French rampages took place in my native country, Côte d'Ivoire. Businesses and private homes were ransacked, and eight thousand foreigners, mostly French, evacuated the country. The only school I had ever gone to back home, from kindergarten to high school, was burnt to ashes by an angry mob. I was a senior at Wesleyan University, applying for jobs, scrambling to get my academic work done and to convince my thesis advisor that I did have a valid topic, and trying to maintain a decent social life. I wasn't sure what to think of the rampages until I started getting e-mails inciting hatred against the "French who had financed rebels and would not let Ivorians govern themselves." I knew then. Words started flowing, questions mostly, unanswered mostly. I called out to everyone I knew, begged them to stop and think, to start verifying their sources of information, to stop spreading propaganda. I had never written a political article before, but my pain and sorrow made it easy.

I was surprised at the volume of responses. Friends from high school, middle school, French, Ivorian, and mixed, wrote back. Some said they were feeling helpless in front of all the destruction and hatred and that they regained some courage by reading my e-mail. Some asked me if they could forward my message to their own contacts. One friend told me that he had received my e-mail from four different sources within a couple of hours. He added that I should consider running for president and that he would vote for me! At that point, I understood that being a leader did not necessarily entail doing extraordinary things all the time. Sometimes, just an e-mail is enough. I had managed to get my point across efficiently and passionately and, even better, as my friends pointed out, I had started a whole new debate.

That episode also highlighted some of my weaknesses as a leader. For example, my passion could become detrimental if not supported by facts and if it remained the only guide of my actions. Also, remote leaders have never been that effective. I was so far from the main action that I could not possibly understand local people's frustrations. That experience showed me the sky and its limits, the shortcomings of my current position, and my abilities as a leader.

ANALYSIS

Few of us will find ourselves in as tragic a situation as did this author, but her message is universal: small actions can have large consequences. This takeaway only resonates, however, because of the emotional connection and authenticity the author establishes with the reader. Stylistically, she mixes long, compound sentences with short, direct ones. It's almost like she's a track runner sprinting with emotional energy, stopping every so often to take short breaths. Her writing is unfiltered and, thus, creates a strong connection with her audience. To say the least, this makes her story more memorable.

To improve upon the essay, the author could have mentioned earlier how she "directed her passion with facts" because it is not self-apparent. In fact, her entire response to the situation appears to be directed by emotion. Would this not mean, in the context of weakness discussion, that her actions "could become detrimental"?

While this loose end slightly undermines her point, she does a great job of otherwise stepping away from the storytelling in the final paragraph to objectively critique her leadership style. With such an emotionally charged topic, it would have been easy to max out the word count to provide more colorful details, but she reserves the appropriate air time for introspection and analysis. Make sure to do this, even if you have to abridge that life-changing story.

II. UNDERGRADUATE EXPERIENCE

What would you like the MBA Admissions Board to know about your undergraduate academic experience?

So you were eighteen when you went to college. Young, impressionable, and experimental—you just wanted to have a good time. Also, you probably did not select your college or courses to justify them to the HBS admissions committee, did you? Besides, come on, that was such a long time ago! Why does the HBS admissions committee want to know about your academic experience? You do not even remember where the diploma is now. No, this essay question is not intended to penalize you for those frat parties and spring breaks years ago.

This essay topic seeks to mine the defining moments of your undergraduate journey. Before you take a stab at this essay, step back and try to think about the following questions. What made you select your undergraduate major? What made you switch course? A move from biology to philosophy is drastic and probably merits an explanation. What are some of your memorable moments, regrets, and takeaways from your undergraduate experience? How did the experience shape your career? Would you do anything differently if you could relive the experience? Remember your audience. For instance, if you already have an undergraduate business degree, how do you think an MBA would add value for you? This is also a great essay to discuss any grade deficiencies and steps you have taken to plug holes in your academic career.

It is tempting to copy and paste undergraduate awards and laurels from your resume. There are plenty of other places in the application to do so, and you will be doing yourself a disservice if you spend valuable word count creating laundry lists. You only have four hundred words, so it may be impossible to throw in everything, including the kitchen sink. Select the undergraduate memories and experiences that have made you who you are today. Not every applicant graduated magna cum laude. But if you did, don't just state the achievement; explain *why* that particular award was important to you.

—Aastha Gurbax and Uma Subramanian

John Coleman

I first considered applying to Berry College while dangling from a fifty-foot Georgia pine tree, encouraging a high school classmate, literally, to make a leap of faith. Every autumn, my school's graduating seniors took a three-day trip to Berry to bond on the ropes course, talk about leadership, and speak frankly about the future, and it was on that retreat, after the ropes course, that I made my own leap.

I had narrowed my college choices to my top scholarship offers, but after a number of campus visits I still hadn't found a place that truly felt like *home*. On the retreat, I realized Berry College was different. The students I met were practical, caring, and curious. The 28,000-acre campus was idyllic. The atmosphere was one of service, leadership, and intellectual curiosity (as founder Martha Berry termed it, an education of the "whole person . . . the head, the heart, and the hands"). Berry also offered what I thought was the best opportunity to mold my own academic experience, take diverse leadership roles, and change myself and my college community in the process.

That is exactly what I did. Taking a "case method" approach to my undergraduate education, I complemented every academic lesson with a practical application. I supplemented my formal education in economics, government, and political philosophy with cigar shop chats, competitive international fellowships, leadership in student government, and in-depth academic research. Rather than studying communication, I practiced communication. As a freshman, I was the campus's top new television reporter, and as a junior and senior, I translated that passion for human connection into a stint as Berry's top newspaper opinion columnist and a widely read campus poet. I was the lead in a one-act play and led my college speech team to its highest ever national finish. I learned business, finance, and organizational leadership by founding a community soup kitchen and leading the campus investment group to unprecedented stock market returns; and in everything, I sought not simply to become better educated, but better rounded—a "whole" person—and to change my campus community in the process.

At Berry, I learned that you can stand trepid before a challenge, transition, or experience. Or you can embrace new challenges, define your own experience, and make a leap of faith. I am proud that my undergraduate academic experience was a period lived in leaps.

ANALYSIS

First of all, this essay is evidence that you do not have to graduate from an Ivy League school to secure admission at HBS.

This essay is a fantastic illustration of how to convey personality through narrative style and diction. John's essay has flair. The essay is successful because readers can get a flavor of what the author would probably be like in real life—restless, action-oriented, and multifaceted.

John is in touch with himself as he explains his choice of school. As he delves further into what makes him tick, he takes a risk in listing a seemingly endless group of activities. However, the stylistic choice works for him as it accentuates his passion and energy. Without stating it outright, the author makes it clear that he would be a colorful addition to HBS, and that attending HBS would be a major step in his personal development. The concluding paragraph is the crowning touch and is consistent with the author's personality and verve.

When writing this essay, avoid creating a shopping list of achievements that can be easily gleaned from other parts of the application. This essay comes dangerously close to doing that but is saved by its vivacious tone and a well-crafted conclusion. It is crucial to unravel your undergraduate experience through the lens of introspection, action, and results. The result itself, however, is less important than what you have taken from the experience. In order to make a lasting impression, your essay must depict a clear picture of what steps you took to shape your undergraduate experience, why you took those steps, and how are you a different person as a result of the experience.

Maxwell Anderson

I like to joke that I chose to study history in college as a career move. After all, history is a growing field. The truth is, I studied history because I love stories. When we incorporate the experiences of our lives into stories, we give them meaning. The stories I learned in college were the most meaningful parts of my education.

I chose my major after encountering Thucydides' *History of the Peloponnesian War*. I had enrolled in a rigorous series of five interdisciplinary courses to read the great works of Western philosophy, history, and literature from antiquity to the modern period. Known among students as "philosophical boot camp," this application-only program required a thousand pages of reading each week. Despite the volume, certain stories refused to be skimmed, and Thucydides' history was a page-turner. Filled with complexity, it continually forced me to reevaluate my own predictions about how the Athenians would react to the looming conflict with Sparta. The dog-eared, scribbled-on pages of my paperback remind me of how the enjoyment of wrestling with the story convinced me to study history.

In my junior and senior years, I wrote three major independent research papers, all of which shared a single broad theme: the political consequences of communications technology revolutions. These projects taught me how to research, evaluate conflicting evidence, and write analytically. They taught me how to write stories myself.

My thesis was a 112-page study of Richard Nixon's successes and failures as an improbable pioneer of televised politics. His story taught me that effective persuasion depends not only on having the right message, but choosing the right venues to communicate the message. It also taught me that, even with a winning message delivered by the right medium, a leader's integrity is what determines his destiny.

Ironically, of all the stories I learned in college, my favorites were not told in the history department, but in an engineering course, High-Tech Entrepreneurship. Taught by a former HBS professor, it introduced me to the case method of learning through stories. I was challenged to form opinions with limited data and debate the best path forward in the uncertain situations confronting the cases' entrepreneurial protagonists. I loved it. It was like reading Thucydides again. Ever since that class, I have thought that two years of full-time case study in business school would be an invaluable professional culmination of my education in history.

ANALYSIS

Maxwell is a history major who likes stories—reading them, dissecting them, and writing them. The entire essay is a web of stories netted together with clear transitions and turning points. The essay is unique because of this alternative approach and its emphasis on self-reflection.

Note that Maxwell explains what made him study history but opts not to discuss his choice of institution. This is not the norm, but it draws the reader into his world of influences and turning points. It also reinforces an essay that shows how the "small" choices we make—like taking a class that reads Thucydides—can be as transformational as the "big" choices.

Although Maxwell presents a powerful synthesis of lessons learned from these undergraduate experiences, the biggest critique of this essay is that while he likes stories, he is unable to make a tangible link between that passion and his success. A sentence or two to solidify the link between his love for stories and how that has led to his competencies and success would make this essay a complete success.

Lavanya Anantharman

Attending an all-woman's institution has instilled in me the self-confidence, the self-assuredness, and the core belief that, as a woman, I can excel in any field that I choose to pursue. In every sphere of my college experience, Smith College ingrained these values in me and has shaped me into the woman that I am today.

Smith's liberal arts curriculum encouraged me to explore a variety of academic fields. I supplemented my study of economics with diverse courses in fields such as religion, music, and history, which sharpened my ability to think analytically and broadened my perspective. My classes were small in size which allowed my professors to focus on my intellectual development, pushing me to take initiative and assert my opinion in a coherent and rational manner, as well as to be receptive to my classmates' points of view.

I also had the opportunity to meet some of the most amazing women that I know today. Through my classes, extracurricular activities, and Smith's unique housing system, I met highly accomplished, diverse women, each striving to achieve manifold professional pursuits. I have spent my childhood growing up in several different developing countries where I always saw a clear disparity between the two genders. My interaction with my peers at college taught me to disregard any stereotypes associated with women. My fellow Smith classmates were planning to pursue careers in an array of different fields, and I sincerely believed that women could thrive in any profession that they choose to pursue.

The Smith alumni network only furthered these beliefs. During the course of my undergraduate studies, I interacted with highly successful alums who have reached the top of their fields. I met Smith alums who are leading doctors, bankers, medical researchers, scientists, and philanthropists, and this allowed me to find my mentors and role models. Rochelle Lazarus, CEO of Ogilvy & Mather; Ann Kaplan, former partner at Goldman Sachs; and Caren Byrd, one of the first female bankers at Morgan Stanley, cultivated in me the drive and inspiration to pursue a career on Wall Street.

Being in an all-women's institution was enriching, empowering, and transformational. My classes, professors, peers, and alums helped me grow and mature and instilled in me a tremendous amount of self-confidence in my abilities and potential. Most importantly, Smith College molded me into a stronger, more self-assured woman with a passion and drive to succeed.

ANALYSIS

From the opening sentence, Lavanya's essay is distinctive, in large part because she chooses to focus on gender, a tactic that grabs the reader's attention. In the first two paragraphs Lavanya describes her experiences at Smith College and very literally walks us through the ins and outs of her college experience.

The greatest strength of Lavanya's essay is its consistency and focus around a particular theme, in this case gender. This essay question is designed to be incredibly wide open. Consequently, many applicants flounder when they try to convey too much in their responses. Implicitly, in pursuing a broad response to the question they fail to tell us something new about themselves. Lavanya targets her message, facing this challenge head-on. She should rest assured that those reading this essay will walk away knowing something that could not be conveyed elsewhere in the application.

Rosita Najmi

With the motto *Pro humanitate,* Wake Forest provided a context for continuing my commitment to service while taking on new academic challenges. With a curriculum that included service-learning—applying classroom lessons to volunteer work—my academic experience involved more than textbooks and lectures. The courses I enjoyed most were untraditional in format, and my classrooms extended beyond a Winston-Salem campus.

During an economics course and subsequent independent study in West Africa, I researched microfinance and later presented my now-published findings to an economics course and to an international conference. When building a school in Vietnam, I understood lessons from politics and history in a new, deeper way. Taking lecture notes in French for a blind classmate allowed me to use my language skills in a service capacity. Finally, by participating in a Model UN course and conference, I had the chance to assess my understanding of the United Nations. My academic experience took place on different continents and in varied languages.

The overlap of disciplines inherent in my liberal arts education prepared me for a postgraduate year of volunteer work at a nonprofit that seeks justice for victims of gender-based persecution. A sociology class on marriage and family, a political science course on human rights, and an English course exploring female subservience and rebellion equipped me with theories, case studies, laws, and anecdotes that I drew upon in fulfilling my duties. Other courses such as philosophy and a writing seminar honed more universally applicable skills in critical thinking and communication, respectively. Making such interdisciplinary connections was stimulating and valuable.

Highlights of my academic experience also included more informal moments. I recall the office hours I shared with an economics professor discussing visions of my vocation that resulted in the selection of both my major and career. I likewise will never forget the image of an English professor's office floor blanketed with small pieces of paper, each a component of a paper I was reorganizing. All of these moments—classroom experiences, extracurricular activities, and volunteer work—formed an interdisciplinary learning experience that sparked professional interests in international development and graduate business education. Harvard's case-study approach well fits my preferred style of learning. Although I entered college as a declared business major, my undergraduate education yielded an economist who remains committed to service, continues to seek academic rigor, and pledges a career to a school motto and personal credo: *Pro humanitate*.

ANALYSIS

This essay is memorable because while it highlights her commitment to social causes and describes her intellectual, social, and geographical interests, it also demonstrates the author's personal development through practical encounters.

Rosita's essay is also strong because it presents a tight thesis and drives home key messages. Notice that she doesn't try to tackle too much. She shows the power in focusing on one takeaway from her undergraduate experience—something that really adds depth. Then we see her personal development through the essay.

Rosita also understands her audience well. In a few short paragraphs, she implicitly creates a connection to Harvard Business School's mission "to educate leaders who make a difference in the world." Given her examples, the connection comes across as authentic.

Rosita could have strengthened her essay by adding more color to her school-building experience in Vietnam instead of adding to a catalogue of unconnected snippets, which distracts the reader from her *Pro humanitate* focus. As it is, the reader is left wanting to understand more about her experiences. Perhaps she could have used an entire paragraph to expand upon one of the brief anecdotes. Nonetheless, Rosita succeeds in building her case and standing out.

Faye Iosotaluno

Misconceptions abound about the undergraduate program at Wharton. Rumor has it that its students are all finance geeks and disconnected from the rest of the Penn community. My experience at Penn decidedly did not reflect any of those things. In the pursuit of a dual degree in English and economics, I naturally felt that I was part of a larger academic environment, exposed to a wider range of students, faculty, and opportunities. I proactively took advantage of all my resources to ensure a robust and engrossing academic experience.

One of my most fulfilling undertakings was the opportunity to take my personal interest in literature and translate it into a business context. Working with Wharton professor Daniel Raff, we traced the evolution of the U.S. book publishing industry from a perspective of technology and scale. I added value by not only researching the distribution side of the business, but also by analyzing the drivers of demand, which leveraged the history of popular culture in literature gleaned from my English program. For me, this was particularly engaging because it shed light on how the books I had come to know and love actually got onto the market and into my hands. The multiple and unique perspectives from both management and literary history helped me to see a more dynamic (and personal) picture of the industry.

Through such experiences, I recognized that the formula for successful learning involves elements outside of the traditional classroom.

As a board member of the Joseph Wharton Scholars Society, a group focused on emphasizing the importance of the humanities and sciences within a business education, I was able to highlight the need for academically rooted programs that would encourage collaboration across academic schools, not just within Wharton. The introduction of the annual Shah Lecture Series brought together economic gurus Jeremy Siegel and Robert Shiller to discuss theory and application in a debate environment for the benefit of the entire Penn community. By fostering communication through the sharing of ideas between the speakers and students, I helped to cultivate a setting where academic principles could confront the issues of real-world application.

My varied undergraduate academic experiences allowed me to discover that knowledge was not only acquired in the classroom, but also accomplished by bridging resources across programs and finding opportunities to engage with diverse peers who brought extraordinary perspectives. I walked away from Penn with a full and well-rounded education as well as the drive to continue my learning in creative and distinct ways.

ANALYSIS

Faye tells her relatively straight-forward story with a flare that distinguishes it from other undergraduate business major narratives. She first catches the reader's attention by boldly stating that typical assumptions about her and other Wharton undergraduates are wrong. The remainder of the essay serves to prove her point. In writing about the Wharton Scholars Society and the Lecture Series, she touches on her undergraduate leadership experiences while highlighting that she is a well-rounded, interesting applicant.

In using these stories, she may be reiterating points on her resume, but the color and context add a new dimension that could not have possibly popped off her resume. It is imperative to highlight the things that make you a progressive and dynamic applicant, and this is especially important for candidates with traditional business background like Faye, who has passed the test with flying colors.

Anonymous

On the eve of my departure for Harvard, my long-standing neighbor and friend, Jack, told me what he had heard and has since never forgotten from his first day of class: Harvard will lead you into a forest, from which you will spend the next four years finding your way out. I have come to fully appreciate the aptness of that statement. I arrived at Harvard a verdant freshman, passionate about intellectual stimulation, excited by challenges, and cautiously aimed for a career in genetic research. Fascinated by the elegant complexity of how a simple DNA double helix can dictate the creation of an entire human being, I spent freshman year taking courses in genetics from both scientific and social perspectives. That spring, I chose to major in biochemistry. By the end of sophomore year, I was three courses away from a degree in biochemical sciences, and I had received As in all my concentration classes. Yet, at the beginning of junior year, I started to reconsider a career in scientific research.

I spent sophomore summer studying Japanese in Hokkaido, and in doing so, realized my interest in international relations. The next summer, I applied for an internship at the U.S. State Department and experienced diplomacy firsthand. My interest in science was enduring, but my ability to understand Chinese and Japanese languages and cultures was an asset I did not want to waste. In the beginning of senior year, I had to make an important decision: Should I pursue an honors thesis in biochemistry, or seize my last chance to access some of the world's finest resources and professors in Japanese studies? I opted for the latter. Life was too short to let such chances pass me by.

Today, I am intensely grateful for having gotten to know, both professionally and personally, some of the most brilliant minds in Japanese literature. Looking back on my four years at Harvard, I can confidently claim that I have no regrets. I walked into the forest, believing my path was clearly laid out for me, only to have discovered a completely different trail. Yet, I am happy to have seen more of the forest before I came out, for when I finally stepped back into the world, I saw a subtler and more exquisite beauty as a result of my explorations.

ANALYSIS

The author of this essay uses the topic to both enhance his image as a person with diverse interests and provide insight into his varied and unique undergraduate transcript. He comes across as introspective and secure in his choices, and without this context his academic transcript alone might have led a casual observer to believe he was a lost soul. The former description clearly makes for a better applicant profile. This essay's success stems also from the author's effective use of metaphors to explain his journey from a Harvard freshman to a career in international relations. It is important to keep in mind that throughout all of your essays, stylish and colorful writing can bring your accomplishments and personality to life. While you must be substantive, your goal is to convince the reader that what you have accomplished is meaningful to you, not that what you have accomplished is monumental on its own. Here, the author shows how he is able to adapt and follow newfound passions. He shares some of his thought process around making unconventional and sometimes risky choices, changing paths when necessary and taking responsibility for his decisions. The author is open-minded; he is able to course-correct and understands what is more important to him as he matures intellectually and emotionally.

One caution: beware of focusing too much on grades. Here the author mentions them only in passing, but given that grades are already reflected in your transcript, you are better served spending your word count revealing new elements of your personality.

Rohan Nirody

After English and Spanish, business is my third language. At first, I did not recognize it as such; I considered finance, accounting, management, and marketing to be mere skill sets. As my undergraduate years progressed, I uncovered the innumerable linkages among those disciplines, and I ultimately realized that my Wharton education was providing me with a new lens through which to interpret the world—in short, a new language.

My academic experience transcended the boundaries of the classroom, for the language of business is spoken everywhere. I proactively sought out unique internship opportunities, which included coordinating an on-campus marketing program for Atlantic Records, helping to develop fund-raising strategies for Bill Bradley's presidential campaign, and working for a start-up search engine at the height of the dot-com bubble. Through such experiences, it became clear that my knowledge of business could help me to better appreciate music, politics, technology, and other personal interests.

Anita Roddick once asserted that "the language of business is not the language of the soul or the language of humanity. It's a language of indifference . . . of separation, of secrecy, of hierarchy." Nevertheless, as a student in the Huntsman Program in International Studies and Business, I took several courses in public policy and international relations that enabled me to frame my business education in a global context and to understand the ways in which economic policy affects societal welfare. Through courses such as Globalization and Human Rights, which examined how multinational corporations impact developing countries, I learned that business can indeed be the language of humanity.

My experiences during a semester abroad in Chile reinforced this point. There, I interviewed the heads of over fifteen water utilities to investigate how the ongoing privatization of the sector was affecting the price and availability of clean water. Working with a microcredit organization, I helped the patrons of an urban homeless shelter to find financing for an entrepreneurial venture. At every opportunity, I engaged with the community, relying on the common language of business when my less-than-perfect Spanish failed me.

Upon graduation from Penn, I chose to begin my career in private equity, where I felt I would have the optimal resources to further my study of business. Going forward, I seek to enroll in HBS in order to learn from and share my experiences with professors and peers who speak different dialects of the same brilliant language.

ANALYSIS

This essay is striking for its effective thematic use of the "language of business." The opening sentence could be cliché, but in the first few paragraphs the author elegantly explains why business is "the lens" through which he views the world. A word of advice to applicants: if you are going to use imagery to explain your point of view, ensure that you take a few words to explain why this image is relevant. Remember, you are not trying to win a Pulitzer Prize; you are trying to explain to the admissions committee why you are a good candidate for Harvard Business School.

Undergraduate Experience

The author of this essay is also successful at highlighting interesting experiences in his undergraduate education that both add color to his personality and distinguish him from other Wharton undergrads. Having marketed for Atlantic Records, raised funds for Bill Bradley, and worked on clean-water issues in Chile, the applicant portrays himself as someone who has made the most of a diverse set of opportunities. Wouldn't you want to get to know this person better?

Finally, the concluding paragraph of this essay provides a nice connection between the author's undergraduate experiences and interest in HBS. It's definitely not necessary, but reinforces the relevance of the essay.

III. CAREER ASPIRATIONS

What is your career vision, and why is this choice meaningful to you?

So you have spent the last five years trolling the seas in a British naval submarine, have been trading on the floor of the stock exchange, or have just recently graduated from college. Moreover, you have just spent several essays talking about your scintillating experiences of the last decade. Now it is time for you to answer what is arguably the most important question of the application: What do you want to be when you grow up? More precisely: What is your career vision and why do you need a Harvard MBA to achieve it? A well-structured response to this question will address four critical points.

First, what are your short-term and long-term career plans? Second, why is this your chosen path? Before you start writing your response, carefully consider both parts of the question. Do not only state a goal. Provide enough context so that the audience understands your decision-making process. This is especially important for applicants with traditional business school backgrounds who intend to return to their current fields. While it is nice that you still hope to find yourself at a prestigious consulting firm in ten years, ensure that you can articulate what about the job, specifically, really satisfies you. Above all, your career vision must be sincere and credible. If you want to be chairman of the International Red Cross, fine, but ensure that you lay out a reasonable plan to get there.

After you have addressed what you want to do, explain why you need Harvard Business School to achieve your goals. It is important to note that the specificity with which the career question mentions HBS varies from year to year. Just keep your audience in mind when crafting your response, however. Harvard's mission, after all, is "to educate leaders who make a difference in the world." Moreover, beyond the mission, keep in mind that the school has been working to differentiate itself from other business schools in a number of more subtle ways in recent years, launching among other things its Global Research centers and its Healthcare Initiative.

Understanding your audience is useful advice when applying to any business school: make sure you understand the differences between the programs and tailor the response to your school of choice.

The final element that makes a career essay truly exceptional is a sentence or two in which the candidate thoughtfully highlights what he or she would bring to the HBS classroom. When incorporated, this touch proves that the applicant understands that HBS is a collaborative environment, in which the exchange of ideas by people of widely diverse backgrounds is what truly enables learning.

—Uma Subramanian

Jason Kreuziger

My highest career aspiration is to ring the opening bell at the NASDAQ as my company celebrates the successful completion of its initial public offering. My experiences have prepared me to build market-disrupting technology companies fit for public investment, but they have also exposed me to the intangible qualities of successful entrepreneurs. These qualities include the ability to manage, presence to inspire, charisma to lead, and fortitude to persist in the face of challenge. These virtues are represented in the bedrock of Harvard's MBA program. My desire to internalize these qualities is the catalyst that drives me to pursue a Harvard MBA with such conviction. The timing of my application coincides with both my developmental needs and the natural termination of my current position in July 2006.

To achieve these goals, I have focused my academic and professional pursuits in the areas of finance and technology. In addition to my undergraduate majors, my work in the technology group of a San Francisco–based, middle-market investment bank has given me a first-hand view into Silicon Valley's technology incubator and the lives of successful technology entrepreneurs. I have learned revolutionizing technologies ranging from enterprise software applications to price-per-click Internet advertising services. The experience has placed me in close contact with senior executives who share the story of my career aspirations as their own reality. The opportunity to interact with such innovative individuals has been an inspiration, and provided me a first-hand account of what qualities today's entrepreneurial leaders possess.

While these experiences form a solid foundation, an MBA from Harvard is necessary for developing the managerial skills, leadership ability, and influential network necessary to achieve my goals. This assertion was confirmed during my campus visit to Bill Sahlman's entrepreneurial finance class where I observed the case method in action as debate raced from eager hand to eager hand, with each comment seeking to improve upon the discussion. The collaborative energy was tangible, the environment exciting, and the effect impressive. A visit to the Arthur Rock Center revealed a collection of memorabilia from companies founded by Harvard alums, foreshadowing the addition I hope to make. A student lunch with a former tech-start-up CFO ensured me other students will share my goals and enthusiasm, adding vital energy to the MBA experience. I left my campus visit knowing that Harvard Business School is where I want to build the next layer upon my foundation.

ANALYSIS

From the "opening bell," the author's essay grabs the reader and brings him along for the ride, setting a quick, consistent tempo for this essay response. Within the first paragraph he addresses all three critical elements of the essay question: What are your career aspirations? Why do you need an HBS MBA? Why now? Additionally, the pace of the essay and the clarity of the vision demonstrated in that first paragraph give the reader insight into the author's personality.

He appears to be someone on a mission with clear goals and the energy to achieve them.

In the second paragraph, the author cleverly distinguishes himself from other banking applicants. By drawing on the lessons he learned and the role models he met in his professional career, the author portrays himself as a thoughtful team player that would contribute unique experiences to a classroom environment.

The remainder of the essay is spent explaining why an MBA from HBS is vital to the author's career development. In discussing his interactions with HBS, the author demonstrates that he has gone beyond merely visiting campus and witnessing the case method. Rather, he projects sincere enthusiasm for the HBS experience and understands what he hopes to contribute. By doing so, the author puts an exclamation point on an exceptional essay.

Anonymous

When I was an infant, Shanghai's air pollution poisoned my lungs. Severe asthma attacks led to recurring hospitalizations; doctors told my mother I would always be sickly. After moving to Minnesota at age five, however, my asthma disappeared and my respiratory system healed. In 2005, I returned to China, and what I saw saddened me. In Xi'an, state-owned factories running twenty-four hours a day spewed black smoke that stained the entire city. People in Beijing and Shanghai wore surgical masks because of the smog. As a near victim of pollution—and an outdoors enthusiast after years of enjoying Minnesota's natural beauty—I felt a strong personal conviction to improve the situation. Unlike the helplessness I felt as a child struggling to breathe, this time I realized that my business interest and knowledge gave me a way to turn conviction into impact.

Wal-Mart CEO Lee Scott recently said, "There need not be conflict between the environment and the economy." As an environmentalist and management consultant, I wholeheartedly agree. My career vision is to help industrial companies in China incorporate environmentally sustainable practices into their business strategies. While manufacturers traditionally view environmental issues as obstacles, I see significant long-term value in being "green." I'm confident this vision is realistic, because I've already seen benefits from "clean" manufacturing while at the Boston Consulting Group (BCG). On a recent project, my team helped a chemicals company discover that their fastest-growing customers preferred suppliers with environmentally friendly reputations. Consequently, our client started viewing environmental infrastructure as a marketing investment, not a capital cost. I also visited a chemical plant operated by my uncle outside Shanghai and learned that clean-air technologies reduced his energy costs and won him the local community's support. These examples inspire me to lead industrial firms in countries like China, where stakes and opportunities are highest.

My post-MBA path will start at BCG, where I will gain exposure to general industrial operations and have opportunities to employ business and leadership lessons. Afterward, I intend to tackle environmental regulatory compliance issues at a multi-national chemical company. Within ten to fifteen years, I hope to launch my own consultancy, helping companies integrate environmental concerns into business strategy. My career vision stems from a passion rekindled with every breath. Now that I am healthy, I intend to exhaust myself finding practical, sustainable solutions so that my future children can breathe a little easier.

ANALYSIS

With vivid imagery, simple prose, and a clearly articulated vision, the author of this essay is successful at distinguishing himself as much more than your average consultant. From the opening sentence, the reader is hooked as the author paints a picture of why he is uniquely suited to help China in its efforts to go green.

The structure of this essay is noteworthy. The author begins by explaining who he is and by succinctly summarizing his professional view of himself as "an environmentalist and a management consultant." He then highlights a very real problem to which he is passionately devoted. In doing so, he answers a critical question: "Why is this your career vision?" By providing concrete examples of how, as a consultant, he can influence companies to make environmentally friendly decisions, the author renders his career objectives highly credible. He follows with well-considered, short- and long-term goals. Finally, he concludes with two strong sentences, laden with personal meaning.

Though compelling in its own right, this essay fails to address one critical question: Why does the author need an MBA specifically from Harvard Business School? Each MBA program offers a unique value proposition for students, so in your essays highlight why a particular school is best suited to help you achieve your goals.

All told, this essay provides a cogent example of how to distinguish an applicant who is interested in pursuing an otherwise traditional career path.

James Reinhart

Google went from college dorm project to search-engine hegemon in twenty months. It took Steve Jobs only a short while to figure out the stickiness of the iPod. Netflix is adding eighty thousand subscribers a month. In the private sector innovation and adoption happen rapidly. A great idea, capable management, and the unwavering belief that you've either tapped an untapped market or you're creating a new one, inspire constant devotion to pushing the boundaries of what's possible.

Public education is the antithesis of this. We've been doing the same thing, albeit worse now than ever before, for more than a century. The United States now ranks twenty-first out of the OECD's twenty-nine industrial nations in eighth grade math. More than a *million* kids dropped out of high school last year—twice the total population of the city of Boston; worse than that, of those who did graduate high school and enroll in college, roughly 40 percent will need remediation. This bankrupt system is ripe for some creative destruction, and in a small corner of California, in "middle class America," that's what I plan to do.

I imagine an America where our schools can do better, where public-private partnerships, dot-com inspiration, and savvy edupreneurs can revolutionize "the business of education" in America. It's already starting to happen in some areas—KIPP (Knowledge Is Power Program), Aspire, Achievement First, Uncommon Schools—but their theory of change is all wrong. Their "no excuses" approach gives most districts lots of excuses as to why it's not scalable.

At the Beacon Education Network we're going to take the same dollars and demonstrate how district schools can increase efficiency, become more accountable for results, recruit and retain higher-quality teachers, and deliver an improved student experience. It's not just about money. It's about rearranging the allocation of resources to increase productivity and paying attention to the prevailing research (there are just as many inconvenient truths about education as there are about global warming). It's also about reimagining what's possible.

The same way Google, Apple, and Netflix are shining a light on what's possible in the private sector, we need a similar Beacon for improving the management of public education. And that's my dream—first with Beacon, then to the Gates Foundation, maybe to New Schools Venture Fund, and eventually to Capitol Hill. I can't envision a more fulfilling or high-impact career than infusing competition into public education, improving school efficiency, reducing the anti-meritocratic influence of teachers unions, and improving the quality and pay of great teachers.

ANALYSIS

James crafts a very effective essay, marked by passionate intensity and unbending logic. He successfully solves the problem encountered by many nontraditional applicants who must explain why a business career makes sense for them.

In this case, James implicitly parallels the needs of the American education system to those of a well-run business. He achieves this by opening with a general statement on how ideas can turn into thriving businesses. He follows with facts about the U.S. education system, with the direct implication that it is in dire need of new ideas. The introduction sets the stage for his vision of an improved public education system in the United States. Furthermore, James writes compellingly about his views and provides specific actions he believes should be taken, thereby delivering a hopeful yet realistic vision. Moreover, James's passion for education is clear, making the reader want him to realize his vision as it sets the premises for a better future for many. Indeed, James speaks as an impassioned leader who is likely to gather many followers and have a significant impact on communities in which he will live. In doing so, James successfully positions himself as one of the leaders Harvard Business School seeks to educate: leaders who make a difference in the world.

The only critique of this essay is that James spends the entire first paragraph setting the scene for his vision. In an essay limited to four hundred words, every sentence is valuable. James could have benefited from spending a sentence or two describing his background and why an MBA will help him achieve his goals.

Jemine Rewane

My career vision is to positively contribute to private-sector development in Africa by enhancing the efficiencies in our business environment. Inefficiencies such as information asymmetry, low productivity and poor access to credit impede economic growth. My goal is to establish a world-class, Africa-based private equity fund that employs effective management techniques and appropriate capital structures to improve underperforming companies.

I believe weak management and poor leadership compound the effects of the aforementioned inefficiencies and are major impediments to economic development. For instance, in Nigeria, despite the recent quadrupling of revenues to $60 billion, (year over year) in 2005 due to favorable oil conditions, 71 percent of the population still live below the international poverty line. Ventures, like Africa-focused private equity funds, can efficiently mobilize resources and introduce ethical and corporate governance in the private sector and help unlock the economy's latent potential. These funds are positioned to take advantage of increasing foreign investments in Africa, the tremendous resource endowment, low labor costs, and sizeable market demand.

Whilst attending HBS's Africa Business Club Conference, I became more aware of the investment opportunities on the continent and met individuals who share my aspirations to make a difference. An exciting decade lies ahead for Africa. The catalyst for our development is leaders who successfully combine advanced business strategies with the resilience and entrepreneurship of African people to achieve international competitiveness. I intend to be one of these leaders and the Harvard MBA education is vital to making this a reality.

There are established answers to many of Africa's challenges. The HBS case method acknowledges that collective problem-solving and Socratic idea-sharing can lead to optimal solutions to problems as complex as Africa's poverty spiral. Through electives like Venture Capital and Private Equity and International Financial Management, I will learn to effectively evaluate investments in developing countries such as Nigeria and profitably execute my fund strategy.

After HBS I intend to build upon my international investment banking career by joining an emerging-markets private equity fund where I will gain tangible and practical knowledge required to navigate this dynamic sector. I see the successful realization of my career vision as a step toward the economic liberation of Africa, a sequel to the achievement of our political independence in the 1960s. The Harvard MBA program will enhance my capacity to achieve my full potential and give back to my society some of the benefits to which I have been privileged.

ANALYSIS

This essay is a well-informed response by a passionate applicant. Fundamentally, the essay is about private equity. It offers a compelling twist, however, because Jemine intends to use that field to address the inefficiencies of her homeland to "effectively mobilize resources." In a few short paragraphs, this author demonstrates she has a definitive plan for making a difference in the world.

It is important to note the clarity with which Jemine expresses herself. The language is crisp, the grammar impeccable, and the message is clear. She displays a consistent sense of personal vision that is directly linked to her career ambitions. Moreover, she demonstrates a thorough knowledge of HBS by mentioning the Socratic idea-sharing that is so critical to the case method, highlighting her attendance at the Africa Business Conference, and providing examples of classes she hopes to take.

In this essay, the author is true to herself. She is not touching on a cause because it is hot at the moment. This is an important point. To avoid sounding hollow, an applicant's essays must legitimately reflect his or her beliefs.

Anonymous

July 27, 1989, twenty years and one week after the first lunar landing, was the day I decided to fly to the moon. The impetus for that decision was a chance encounter at Space Camp between nine-year-old me and Apollo XVI astronaut Charlie Duke, one of only twelve men to have ever voyaged to the lunar surface. I will forever remember Charlie's speech because it instilled in me a fascination with exploration that continues to fuel my career aspirations.

Today, I am a systems engineer on the Crew Exploration Vehicle (CEV) program, which is chartered with returning astronauts to the moon and, more importantly, with rejuvenating interest in space exploration. The work is inspiring, though not for the reasons I had anticipated. In fact, over the last year, I have realized that what intrigues me is not the development of technical solutions, but rather the loftier ideals, such as making exploration relevant to the average person.

I believe that to be sustainable in today's dynamic, global market, where competing interests vie for every dollar, any major initiative must consistently show value and demonstrate tangible, relevant benefits to its market. Specifically, I think that to survive, the CEV Moon-Mars program must be strategically marketed.

Equipped with an MBA, I hope to lead that effort. In fact, my near-term career aspirations are to work in business development for a CEV contractor and sell the benefits of space exploration to both the American people and international partners. Ultimately, my goal is to lead a firm that develops technologies that enable both government and private space exploration.

I believe that an MBA education from Harvard Business School, where I would learn the science of marketing sophisticated technologies and develop a solid general management foundation, will help me achieve my goals. I am especially interested in classes such as Commercializing Science and Technology and in learning from technology management experts who have tremendous real-world experience. Finally, because I believe that free exchange of ideas is the catalyst for progress, I am excited about collaborating with talented classmates whose passions differ from mine.

If I were to become a member of the HBS Class of 2008, I would return to aerospace just as increasing resource demands will require the exploration initiative to have a champion who understands how to sell big ideas. The timing could not be more perfect.

ANALYSIS

This is a tight, well-structured, and fast-paced essay that encourages the reader to keep reading on. The author grips you with vivid imagery and builds her story in chronological order. She clearly explains the context of her career vision and then specifically articulates what she hopes to do after business school (lead the strategic marketing effort on the CEV program).

She has strong views and is able to convince the reader of her enthusiasm and passion for aerospace. She couples a coherent vision with research on HBS classes and an understanding of the HBS culture. She makes the case that by attending HBS, she would be able to exchange ideas, learn the art of marketing, and interact with peers and experts.

One critique of this essay is that the author could highlight why she wants to do an MBA "now." She mentions that the timing could not be "more perfect" but does not elaborate on why the timing is right. She could also have talked about what she would contribute to the HBS community. A sentence or two in this regard would have shed further light on what kind of person the author is.

Apar Kothari

Each of my experiences has contributed to my long-term goal of working in healthcare venture capital. Growing up in Boston around a family of medical professionals, I have constantly been fascinated by healthcare. My father discussed the medical environment with me every day, leading me to volunteer at local hospitals and attend a Medical Scholar's program. My interest intensified when I developed Hodgkin's lymphoma in 2003.

While working in IBM's VC group, I participated in a number of internal ventures to nurture start-ups to success. I learned the fundamentals of fund management, and have seen the importance of financially supporting innovators who could develop life-changing technologies, such as the transdermal patch, which may soon allow cancer patients to painlessly receive chemotherapy.

A venture capitalist requires not only business skills but also an intense commitment to the goals that these start-ups represent. With my family's background in healthcare, my own ordeal as a patient, and my experience with start-ups at IBM, I have become committed to a life that makes the sum total of my experience available to others. Before transitioning into VC, however, I plan to work in business development in a pharmaceutical company to gain domain expertise and applicable skills. Surviving Hodgkin's has given me a renewed determination to pursue my goals now, and a Harvard MBA will provide me with the structural framework to achieve them.

Through simple observation, I've discovered that MBAs possess an analytical nature that provides them a distinct advantage over those without. In light of my VC bent and family being in Boston, I'm convinced that HBS is indeed my ideal fit for business school. I will learn from faculty of the highest caliber, and acquire skills in qualitative assessment and creative problem-solving. HBS's legacy case method will offer me the ideal training for real-life situations, allowing me to develop a solid framework to work more effectively in VC.

The opportunity to develop a network at HBS will also be invaluable. I have visited twenty-four countries, travel to India every year, and speak Gujrati, Hindi, Spanish, and English. As a result, I appreciate diverse cultures and am eager to further broaden my perspectives by working with my ninety section mates. Additionally, I plan on engaging in the Healthcare Club, Women's Student Association and Ski Club. I am looking forward to a truly transformational experience, which will hone my skills in such a way that I'll be able to use business to improve the quality of life for both specific individuals and in the broader global context. As such, I will be an active contributor not only at HBS but also at destinations that follow.

ANALYSIS

The strength of Apar's response lies in its structure and clarity. Early in the essay, Apar articulates her vision to work in healthcare venture capital. Then, in short order, she addresses the factors that led her to pursue this career path: familial influence, volunteer work, personal health challenges, and prior professional experience.

Without asking for sympathy, Apar highlights her courageous battle with Hodgkin's lymphoma and explains that it has "given [her] the renewed determination to pursue [her] goals now." Apar herein not only addresses the critical timing component of the essay question, but also provides sincere insight into why this career path is meaningful to her. She then smoothly segues into how an MBA fits into her broader career vision and makes a strong case for why HBS is the program best suited for her.

In the fifth paragraph, Apar deviates somewhat from her message when she mentions her language skills and travel history. Although these stories certainly add depth to her personality, she would have been better served by tying these experiences more directly into her career vision, or using the space to specifically outline what she would bring to the classroom environment at HBS. In the broader context of Apar's essay, these are small comments on what is an otherwise tight, well-structured response.

ANONYMOUS

"So, what would I do on a typical day?" the candidate asked. During my own job search I had posed this question to at least half a dozen interviewers—only to be frustrated when each struggled to respond coherently. But I could reply with ease. Right? Wrong. With every word I uttered the interviewee's expression grew increasingly confused. Then it dawned on me: this is not a difficult question, it simply does not have an answer. There is no "typical" day in management consulting, which is why I love working for A. T. Kearney and intend to return upon completing my MBA.

I value that my career exposes me to a variety of industries, corporate cultures, and business issues. Companies I have helped include a family-owned paper products manufacturer, a midsized media conglomerate, and a leading insurance corporation. Immersing myself in an assortment of organizations keeps me engaged and allows me to more rapidly acquire a well-rounded skill set than I might in industry. As a consultant, I have polished my negotiating, modeling, interviewing, and presenting skills—and expect to add many more to this list over time.

Leveraging my strengths is equally important to me as evolving into a more versatile businessperson. Although consultants' day-to-day activities vary, the attributes essential for success in consulting are static: sharp analytical and interpersonal skills. It is no coincidence that these are two of my strongest traits; after all, confidence that I am best equipped for consulting is what initially prompted me to enter this profession. Proud as I am of having been promoted twice, on each occasion after minimum time in grade, what truly motivates me is the prospect of guiding others through fast-paced, perpetual change as a partner.

I am certain that the HBS core curriculum, along with electives such as Leading Professional Service Firms, will unlock my full potential as a consultant and enable me to reach this level. No business could better cater to my desire to be challenged. Problems I solve, with whom I work, how much information I have—all will be in a constant state of flux as long as I am a consultant. The unpredictability of my daily routine is not only what makes any attempt to answer that candidate's question an exercise in futility, but also the most demanding part of the fulfilling career I plan to resume after graduating from HBS.

ANALYSIS

This essay commentary is addressed to applicants with traditional business school backgrounds, such as investment banking and consulting. These candidates often face the difficult challenge of differentiating themselves from similarly distinguished applicants.

What is striking about this response is the author's enthusiasm for his chosen profession. By opening with an interesting anecdote, the applicant draws the reader into his consulting world. While describing his favorite attributes about his career, the author reveals elements of his personality: an insatiable curiosity, a strong willingness to learn, and an ability to succeed in a challenging and dynamic environment. Though his long-term aspiration to be a partner at

A. T. Kearney is not comparatively differential, the author explains clearly why it is the right vision for him. He is straightforward, yet compelling, and succeeds in convincing the reader that, for him, consulting is not merely a job; it is a passion.

Despite its strengths, this essay suffers from an overuse of business lingo. The author mentions "leveraging" his strengths and "unlocking his full potential as a consultant" and in doing so misses opportunities to highlight specific skills that he hopes to gain from an MBA. Additionally, the author does not effectively illustrate how an MBA from HBS fits into his career vision. As it is currently written, the essay could generically be used as part of an application for any school. This is a critical point: know your audience and offer a persuasive argument as to why you are applying to the program you have selected.

Anonymous

I want to become the mayor of Cartagena, a congresswoman in the House and Senate, a cabinet member and, votes permitting, even more. I wish to make a significant impact in my country and I wish to do it through public service.

This choice has been a longtime goal, and my work with the Colombian government has only served to confirm it. I would like to help Colombia grow and prosper, and I believe I have the capacity to make a substantial contribution. I find giving to the country both personally enriching and professionally fulfilling, and I think only by doing that can I be truly happy. I am passionate about Colombia and the decisions I have made throughout my life have been geared toward better preparing myself to serve it.

I attended Exeter and Harvard, for instance, because I yearned for a very rigorous education. I took a year off between one and the other to learn about Colombia at the University of the Andes and to strengthen my social network while there. I worked at Dove Consulting to develop valuable strategic thinking skills and I returned to Colombia to follow the path of my chosen career. Finally, I decided to work at the National Planning Department of Colombia (DNP) because it was a fertile training ground for future leaders and because it would acquaint me with the economic and political realities of the country.

I would like to pursue an MBA because I want to become a

well-rounded leader in the public sector and I need to build the skills I am still missing: finance, accounting, economics, general business administration, and a solid understanding of the private sector. Despite the importance of correct business management in government, the latter is sparse among my peers. There is more to government than policy, and yet few—myself included—are trained to take on much beyond that. Although an MPA/MPP would no doubt also be useful, those programs would develop competencies I already have and would not necessarily delve upon those still foreign.

Through politics I want to make a meaningful difference in Colombia, and the transformational leadership training provided by an HBS MBA will be pivotal in that quest. HBS's extensive network of Latin American alumni, its Buenos Aires Research Center, its Latin American Business Conference, and its proximity to the Kennedy School of Government will furthermore connect me to the region's current and future leaders and help me understand the interplay between business and government.

ANALYSIS

This applicant's essay is striking for the boldness with which it communicates her vision. In no uncertain terms, the author states that she hopes to lead her country, Colombia. This essay is well structured in that it explains where the author is coming from, where she hopes to go, and why she needs an MBA specifically from Harvard Business School. In discussing HBS, the author shows that she has done her homework and has learned about aspects of the school that truly differentiate it from its competitors.

There is one weakness in this response, however. Because the author does not mention the specific steps that she intends to take to achieve her vision, there is a credibility gap in the essay. The audience is left thinking: It is great to hope to run a country, but how does the author intend to get there? What are her immediate post MBA goals? In the fourth paragraph, rather than articulating why she is not pursuing a public policy degree, the author would have been better served to lay out a clear plan for the future. The reference to a road not taken is an unnecessary digression from the author's main point.

Ultimately, this essay is a persuasively written, passionate testament from a motivated candidate with a bold and different career vision that distinguishes her from other applicants.

Stephen Cravens

I have a passion for energy. No other industry is as far-reaching in its impact on the world. Energy enables public and private sector development, it influences the rise and fall of nations, and it even transforms societies and the everyday lives of the individuals that constitute them. By providing the capital to finance infrastructure, exploration, and technological development related to energy, I believe I can have the greatest impact in the global arena. My long-term goal is to become managing partner at an international private equity firm focused on the energy industry.

Working alongside entrepreneurial management teams who flourish amid the flexibility of the private equity business model excites me. On a daily basis, I see opportunities to do things that just are not available in other specialties—creative ideas to stretch our limits for what can be accomplished. Whether investing in a company that generates electricity from waste in landfills or one that extracts difficult-to-recover, unconventional natural gas in China, firms such as First Reserve are at the forefront of innovative structures and unexploited opportunities.

To help me achieve this vision, the key next step is a graduate business education. An MBA is fundamental to advancing to management-level positions in private equity and will equip me with the competencies to meaningfully improve organizations. Whether managing an investment firm or stepping in to run a struggling portfolio company, the functional and managerial knowledge that an HBS education furnishes will give me confidence to lead effectively in various situations.

During a campus visit in April, I sought out the HBS faculty members most germane to my career vision. I spoke with Richard Vietor on energy policy and with Nabil El-Hage on the private equity form of corporate governance. Through discussions with students, I realized that HBS is the ideal place for me to meet my future private equity partners and industry peers.

Attending Mukti Khaire's Entrepreneurial Management class, I saw the case method performed live from the front row. Observing the lightning-fast class discussion, I am confident there is no better training ground for me to develop the skills necessary to drive meaningful change in the organizations on which I have an influence. For the skills that I will develop, and for all that I can and will contribute, I view Harvard Business School as the most valuable MBA program I could attend.

ANALYSIS

Stephen's passion and his clear understanding of HBS set him apart from his private-equity peers. Initially, Stephen draws the reader in with a dramatic statement, "I have a passion for energy," and follows with an articulately crafted paragraph about why he believes energy is so vital to the world economy. He demonstrates thorough knowledge about the industry and in the second paragraph highlights how his work experiences have helped shape his worldview.

After articulating his vision, Stephen addresses two other critical elements of this prompt. To answer the question "Why an MBA,"

Stephen highlights the specific relevance of the degree to success in private equity. In addressing "Why HBS," Stephen clearly demonstrates that he has taken initiative to get to know the school.

What is also noteworthy for future applicants is the way in which Stephen speaks to his audience. He takes a traditional goal—to be a partner in a private equity firm—and encases it in a vision that would enable him "to make a difference in the world," thus demonstrating an implicit understanding of the HBS mission.

Similar to the critiques of other essays in this section, Stephen could have strengthened his case by highlighting specific skills he hopes to develop at HBS, thus proving that the education is not merely career enhancing. He could have also discussed what he will bring to the HBS classroom, and what he will contribute to the community.

Anne Morriss

I have watched the world change around people who were unprepared for its transformation. I have defined "commodity" for Brazilian coffee brokers whose market suddenly seemed to ignore them. I have argued about Mercosur with a tired finance minister in Ecuador, and have seen Dominican friends fight for jobs in a new *zona franca* condemned by international labor groups.

I want to help clarify the confusion, and I want the Harvard Business School to be my ally.

I am choosing HBS for the traditional outputs. I want to increase my impact on organizations, to join a network of people with the courage to reach difficult goals, to gain unmatched credibility as a messenger. HBS has an outstanding reputation for offering these things, and my research confirms it. Most of the HBS students and alumni I know are expanding their definitions of greatness.

I also want the journey. I want the daily luxury of exploring the world with the extraordinary community that HBS builds. I want to engage Frances Frei on my company's failed technology dream and see Haitian competitiveness from Michael Porter's perspective. I want to argue with James Austin about the private sector's ability to drive social change and discuss the responsibilities of corporations with exceptional peers who will translate their convictions into meaningful action.

I came to ontheFRONTIER to learn to fight poverty in a new

global context. I want to advance that fight, and I want to test and improve my strategy at HBS, a place that will hold me to the highest standards of analysis and tutor me in the messy art of leadership.

ANALYSIS

This poetic essay grabs your attention from the get-go. It snubs the traditional thesis-plus-evidence structure and craftily spins the rationale for pursuing an MBA at HBS. Most striking still is the passion that Anne exudes for impacting the world around her.

While not stated outright, and even without the context of the entire application, the reader can deduce Anne's ambitions to continue in her field of economic development. She describes her past experience through expressive snippets of her work in emerging markets. These accounts are ever more powerful because of the personal touches she colors them with—a conversation with Ecuador's finance minister, friends seeking employment in the Dominican Republic—and despite all these global accomplishments, she makes a strong case for returning to school for an MBA.

While Anne dedicates more words to HBS than we would recommend, she succeeds in providing incisive examples of why HBS is her school of choice. She has obviously done background research and is familiar with the faculty and their work. In the process, she exposes her own personal interests and motivations. The strength of this essay lies both in the nobility of Anne's goals and in the eloquence of the delivery. The reader is convinced through Anne's well-expressed convictions that she will be a powerful agent of change.

IV. TYPICAL DAY

While recognizing that no day is typical, describe a representative day.

This is an essay question that at first glance seems almost too easy: describe a typical day. How hard can that be? Do not be fooled; this is a question worth spending some time on, one that if done well can communicate a great deal about your personality and how you approach the world and solve problems.

The chronology of what you do and the hour-by-hour specifics of your diary are not all that important. What matters here is how you choose to say what you say. To simply list what you do is not going to win you many points. Your resume probably covers most of what you do (or should, anyway), so this is your chance to demonstrate why you are good at what you do and what types of experiences you will contribute as a member of the HBS community.

As you will see from the essays we have chosen, there are many approaches that can work. Bending the rules with this essay is okay, so do not feel compelled to describe your day purely chronologically. Many people, though, do exactly that, so if that is how you end up approaching the essay that is fine.

In addition to showing a range of formats that can work, we have tried to pick essays that are especially good at revealing aspects of the author's character and personality. Some are funny but many are not. Some are strikingly well written but, again, many are not. Writing beautifully helps (sometimes a lot) but it is not a prerequisite for admission. What is? The ability to demonstrate perspective, poise, and maturity, all of which are common to all the essays we have chosen.

Most people who apply have done interesting and important things, so simply confirming or reiterating that you, too, have done interesting and important things is not going to distinguish you from the crowd. The key here is not to underestimate what seems like an overly easy question. This is an additional opportunity to help the admissions committee learn more about you and how you view the world.

—Dan Erck

Anonymous

Alarm clock. Clock radio. Cereal. Multivitamin. Rain. No jog today.

The firm represents your career as one pyramid inverted on top of the other. The bottom pyramid represents analysts and associates; the top pyramid, junior and senior partners. At the fulcrum is the case manager. It is the best and worst role at the firm.

Five new voice mails, twelve new e-mails. Scan *Red Herring, Venture Wire, American Banker, WSJ,* and the *NY Times*. Must stay current, I rationalize. Client calls. "Could we have an update before the presentation to review the findings?" The presentation is only four days away. "Absolutely." "I'll see you tomorrow in Parsippany at eight-thirty A.M."

The best part is that you see and do it all. You watch partners agree to outrageous proposals. You design the analysis to execute those proposals. You learn your clients' quirks and earn their confidence. You guide your team. You support the firm, too—writing articles, giving recruiting seminars on "cracking a case interview."

A partner stops by: "I promised Tom that we would incorporate the perspective of Japanese beverage executives." Panic. The analyst reminds you of his vacation. Meet with case team. Reshuffle work plan. Interview client CFO. Rewrite executive summary (again). Gently, have "career concerns" discussion with advisee.

The worst part is that you see and do it all. It is all ultimately your responsibility: the right answer, a happy client, a non-mutinous case team, the partner appearing at the meeting and remembering the topic. You are one part uber-analyst, one part therapist, one part administrative assistant. Secretly, I like this responsibility, too.

What time does the gym close? Business plan needs another iteration. Girlfriend calls: "We are meeting for dinner at nine, right?" Panic. E-mail document to client. Grab a taxi. Rain. Everything will be fine. It always is.

ANALYSIS

If you are a consultant, answering this question can be terrifying. Everyone knows what a consultant does, but here you are trying to describe a typical day in a way that is interesting and that sets you apart from the crowd. It is no easy task, but the writer of this essay passes with flying colors.

Humor helps, as does the author's thoughtful (and honest) perspective of what it is like to be a case manager and balance the myriad demands from coworkers, partners, clients, and life outside of work. The writing is crisp and the pace fast. The end of the essay—"Everything will be fine. It always is."—is a nice touch and says to the admissions committee that the author is not so overwhelmed by day-to-day pressures that he loses sight of the bigger picture and what is really important in life. No matter what your background, demonstrating that you can see your job in a larger context (connecting the dots, so to speak) is invaluable and demonstrates maturity and poise. The takeaway from this essay is that you can tell a very descriptive tale in few words. Do not panic if you are worried you are not an amazing writer. Do spend the time to think about what you do, why you do it well, and how to succinctly convey this along with a bit about your unique personality.

Jay Glaubach

Since graduating from college I have played various roles in various places, including a law student in Boston, a schoolteacher in northern Spain, and an investment banker in New York, London, and Frankfurt. Although it would be impossible to collapse these experiences into a single representative day, I can paint my daily experience with broader strokes. Every day I learned something. Every day I met new people. For these reasons, every day was a challenge.

Every day I learned something new. In Frankfurt I took daily German lessons before work. In New York I learned accounting and corporate valuation on the job. In law school I am learning how to analyze judicial decisions and the policies behind them. Despite the diversity of the past few years, every day has comprised a learning experience.

Every day I interacted with new people from diverse backgrounds. In investment banking I worked with management teams from all over the world, including England, Italy, Finland, and Japan. I argued the merits of the matadors with Spaniards at the bullfights in Madrid. I had dinner with the grandfather of my best friend in Germany, who lived under Hitler's troops in Frankfurt and Khrushchev's in East Berlin. Every day was typified by a unique interaction, however small, with someone who widened my perspective on the world.

Due to these elements, every day has been a challenge. Meeting new people, whether they were clients, coworkers, or classmates, has compelled me to try to understand their distinct viewpoints. Adjusting to new cultural and professional environments has consistently challenged me to readjust my outlook, and staggered me with how much I have yet to learn. My representative day has been alternately frustrating and enrapturing. It has been educational, humbling, enthralling, and demanding. But it has never been boring.

ANALYSIS

This is a wonderful, albeit unconventional essay. Jay is taking a risk here by not describing one single representative day but instead painting a broader picture of how he approaches all days. An essay like this could easily stumble but in this case works beautifully.

Jay has done many things in many cities and wants the admissions committee not to see him as a banker or lawyer but rather as someone who is curious and craves new experiences. Jay is saying to the admissions committee that he will thrive in a diverse place like HBS. Jay's competitive advantage is his breadth of experiences, and the implication that it will contribute to a richer class discussion.

By acknowledging that "every day has been a challenge" and that he is "staggered" by how much he has yet to learn, Jay comes across as humble and approachable. This is critical because if the essay bombs it will be because the tone misses the mark. A key takeaway here is that it is okay to be creative when answering this question. Most people describe a representative day chronologically but as Jay proves, there are other approaches that can work just as well.

Lexie Hallen

Early morning. A genomics laboratory in Germany.

I drop reagent into vials containing my skin cell scrapings and the chief scientific officer nods approval. Due diligence is always engaging, but it rarely provides the opportunity to purify one's DNA. I had asked to experiment with the company's new testing kits in order to evaluate whether the technology is simple enough to permit layperson use, as management touts. This analysis will support my investment case.

I next meet with the company's CEO. We trade fresh biotech gossip and then I challenge the growth rates he is projecting for a new business unit, citing evidence from my own industry analysis. In the past few years I have learned to balance a strong company rapport with the ability to ask tough questions. En route to the airport, I call Fidelity portfolio managers with my revised thesis and downgraded numbers on this company and urge them to sell their stock. As the sole European biotechnology analyst, the portfolio managers rely on my guidance to position their funds.

Back in the London office.

I write a note of thanks in Italian to a company that visited our office the previous week. My U.S. counterpart calls. I had suggested that we share industry insights on a regular basis to help each other pick stocks. Now we are working together to determine whether a recent spate of profit warnings from the life science companies are isolated events or indicative of a slowdown in capital equipment spending.

Prowling the corridors, later that day.

Armed with DCF spreadsheets and Play-Doh, I talk through pipeline assumptions with a dubious fund manager. I construct model antibodies and drug receptors to explain how a Nordic company I want him to buy makes drugs with superior side effects. He calls trading to build a position, and I am pleased with the results of my interactive teaching.

Evening, markets closed. Stocks at rest. I wonder what intrigue they will bring tomorrow. I head home to stir-fry a dinner for friends with my new wok.

ANALYSIS

Lexie does a nice job with this essay by demonstrating that she is a hands-on and curious analyst. Throughout the essay Lexie emphasizes that not only can she run the numbers but also ask tough questions of CEOs and then explain complex technologies to fund managers back at the home office. She is engaged in her work but not so deeply so as to lose the necessary perspective to evaluate companies. This maturity is what distinguishes Lexie from the hundreds of other equity analysts who apply to HBS each year. Instead of just saying, "This is what I do," Lexie takes it to the next level and demonstrates why she thinks she is more capable than other applicants with similar backgrounds.

The tone of the essay is confident but not condescending and says to HBS: "This is why I am good at what I do—pick me!" You can tell Lexie takes pride in what she does and believes she is helpful to her colleagues. The take-home message here is, do not shy away from saying you are good at what you do. Be careful how you say it, however. Do not be arrogant; be humble and demonstrate why you are good at your job and why what you do every day is relevant in a broader context.

Benoit-Olivier Boureau

In charge of logistic developments for five Asian factories, I manage project teams for systems implementation and coordinate with local operational teams to make supply chain improvements. I also manage the overall logistics activity of the strategic products manufactured in Asia. These different functions provide an interesting combination of diverse short-term and midterm issues that make no day typical. And today was a representative day.

I started with a phone call to the managers of projects in China and the Philippines. Through these daily reviews I assist them in their difficulties, and we define corrective actions that are followed up the next day.

Mornings are usually kept for operational issues that need to be tackled during the day with Asian teams. Today, while shaking hands with the logistics staff of the Bangkok factory, a fault in the invoicing system was reported to me, and I helped to analyze the cause. Later, along with the quality department, I examined a customer complaint and decided to freeze shipments of a product to check the stock quality.

Lunch was an opportunity to brainstorm with Thailand's production manager on the potential flexibility of a new machine. We planned a meeting to detail the stock savings expected.

Because of the time difference, I usually dedicate afternoons to midterm issues for which I have strong interactions with the French headquarters. Today I consulted with marketing regarding the decision to cease production of a product made in Thailand. Then, after a review with the industrial strategy department, I finalized a machine investment midterm plan for the Philippines, in preparation for a business trip there.

My evenings are also active, with dense social life. Today I took a colleague to the opening of my Chinese friend's painting exhibition.

ANALYSIS

The inescapable conclusion from reading Benoit-Olivier's essay is that his days are filled with making decisions and resolving problems across multiple countries and time zones. Without bragging, he conveys the extent and gravity of the responsibility resting on his shoulders. The essay portrays him as a flexible manager, able to make judgment calls on the spot when necessary, but willing to consult matters when more significant repercussions are likely. He comes across as someone able to communicate and work across linguistic and cultural barriers who is respected as a manager for his maturity and extensive experience. All of those aspects make him an attractive candidate and a valuable potential contributor to the diversity at HBS.

If anything, Benoit-Olivier could have improved his conclusion. The very brief references to a social life and his interest in art lack substance a little. Including additional details about these aspects of his life—even if they are not relevant professionally—could have provided further insight into his already well-rounded personality and character.

Jason Bohle

A Day in the Life

7:30 A.M.: Alarm clock blares with The Beatles: "Wake up. Get out of bed. Drag a comb across my head. Catch the bus in seconds flat." Perform said lyrics.

8:00 A.M.: Catch train, skim the headlines of the *WSJ* and then delve into the international section. Get so absorbed almost miss my stop.

9:00 A.M.–12:00 NOON: Review cash flow and valuation analyses prepared by members of the Latin American team. Work with team to confirm growth assumptions and discuss sensitivity of investor returns to currency assumptions.

1:00 P.M.: Call investment bankers or officers of an investment target and ask questions about inconsistencies or confusing aspects of the financial models they provided. Ask for updates on previously requested questions or documents.

2:00 P.M.: For a different deal, field a curve ball thrown by the target company's lawyers. Work with these lawyers and our counsel to analyze and discuss the effects of proposed changes in the legal and tax structure of the transaction.

3:00 P.M.: Call CEO and CFO of target company to tell them what progress we have made and what we still need from their bankers or management team. Brainstorm with them on solutions to comments made by the lawyers. Outline steps for the next few days.

4:00 P.M.: Meet with my supervisor and the Latin American team. Update them on my progress and highlight any key outstanding issues or pressure points that must be resolved.

4:30 P.M.: Begin gathering and processing information that will be presented to our investment committee in a few weeks.

6:30 P.M.: Plan goals that need to be accomplished for tomorrow's ten-day trip to Mexico and Brazil.

7:00 P.M.: Start home. Read.

8:00 P.M.: Run five miles, watching sunset along the Hudson River.

9:30 P.M.: Meet friends for dinner, jazz show, or a movie.

ANALYSIS

This is a straightforward, solid essay that does not try to blow you away with superhuman feats, but rather establishes Jason as a hard worker who manages to maintain a reasonably balanced life despite being in a high-stress, fast-paced industry. The best line in the essay—and the one that makes you think Jason is probably a pretty good guy—is the first one about performing The Beatles' lyrics. It is a good (and funny) opening and sets a relaxed tone for the rest of the essay. Everything that follows is a fairly standard description of a day in the life of a banker. Nonetheless, Jason's incorporation of a consistent set of references to Latin America and international affairs helps him stand out a little from the group of his investment banking peers.

While overall this essay does a good job describing a typical day,

Jason could have added a little more depth to it. He could have peppered his day with stronger instances of taking a leadership role or simply added more introspective details. Nevertheless, you do not have to hit a grand slam with all of your essays to make a good impression. In fact, forcing world-beating essays out of thin air across the board will probably help you a lot less than just answering some of the questions simply and matter-of-factly. That is what Jason has done here and it worked well for him.

V. THREE ACCOMPLISHMENTS

What are the three most substantial accomplishments, and why do you view them as such?

While the other essay topics may change somewhat year to year, this essay continues to be a permanent fixture in the HBS application. With a more generous word limit of six hundred words, it offers a unique opportunity to tell the admissions committee what is most important to you as an individual and as a professional.

Many applicants have trouble identifying their most significant accomplishments. You may wonder if your achievements are significant enough. It is expected that college students with a few years of work experience will not have restructured a Fortune 500 company or received a Nobel prize. Achievement, however, does not need a grandiose setting. It can be taken from parenthood or interaction with peers. Admissions officers want your achievement to be relevant to *you* before it is relevant to anyone else. Ask yourself the following questions when selecting your accomplishment: Can I convince the reader that this achievement is worthwhile to me, not that it is ground-breaking in its own right? Did I make a meaningful impact to my life through this accomplishment? Will these accomplishments complete a picture of the larger person that I am?

Applicants also find that sharing their stories is not easy—they can be too personal, too long ago and hard to communicate. Try to open up in this essay. What has made you happy and proud in your life? What makes you tick? Be original. Be honest. For some authors, accomplishment takes place in the context of parenthood. For others, it manifests itself in guiding an entrepreneurial family-owned company. In one of the selected essays, accomplishment took shape through conquering bulimia.

There are no set rules, but most applicants allocate roughly two hundred words to each accomplishment. Many applicants stick to the safe but overused template of one academic achievement, one professional achievement, and one extracurricular achievement. Do not feel compelled to do so—the essays that follow a different format can be more lively and memorable.

This essay requires introspective analysis within a meaningful personal context. The point of this essay is not to simply brag about an award you won at college or a mountain you hiked. Remember that the actual result is in many ways less important than your thoughts and actions and what you have taken away from the experience.

—Aastha Gurbax

Anonymous

In the earliest days of my first job out of college, I fought through a major setback and achieved a position of significant responsibility. I joined Senator John Kerry's presidential campaign as the assistant to the communications director, but two days after I arrived, my boss quit. I was reassigned as a volunteer to stuff envelopes and answer phones. My high hopes for a challenging and exhilarating experience were deflated and I found myself both literally and figuratively in the basement, with no apparent exit. Yet, I was passionate about the campaign's goals and determined to make the strongest impact possible. So, while performing the basic tasks asked of me, I sought out additional opportunities, fostered friendships throughout the staff, and demonstrated that I was reliable, hard-working, cheerful, and cooperative. Within a month, I was hired into the fund-raising department, and shortly thereafter, I was promoted to be the campaign manager's executive assistant. This accomplishment was transformative. I learned the importance of experiencing a setback without dwelling on my disappointment. I learned to temper my impatience to fuel my determination rather than to sap it. I learned to measure my talents without exaggerating them. I found that I had the capacity to network effectively across age ranges and responsibilities. I gained insights into good management and effective leadership. And I gained confidence in my ability to turn a dispiriting setback into a meaningful experience.

Following a promotion to product manager at CashEdge, I led a ten-person, cross-functional team on a six-month project to develop a new product to help small businesses process payables and receivables electronically. The product is being resold through Bank of America, and we just inked a deal with Microsoft to build the product into its forthcoming Vista operating system to enable payment applications on the desktop. This achievement stands out in my mind for the following reasons: I successfully delivered an innovative and compelling product with only fourteen months' experience in the technology industry. I demonstrated that I could effectively sell a product to a variety of business and technical audiences at major corporations. The deal with Microsoft is a significant step in CashEdge's drive to go public, and contributing to that effort feels great. I also realized that product management, which blends the creativity and initiative required for product development with the excitement of working directly with clients, mirrors the experience of starting a company and is an excellent training ground as I develop the skills necessary to launch my own company.

Within four months of publishing our book privately in November 2005, my partner and I surpassed $20,000 in sales, moved into the black, and sold the national publication rights to Nation Books. *Actions Speak Louder Than Bumper Stickers* (*ASLTBS*) is a collection of humorous political bumper stickers accompanied by sobering facts that ground the punch lines in reality. The idea came to me in August 2005—too late to sell the concept to a publisher and have it distributed by the holidays. So, with a $10,000 self-funded investment, and while continuing our full-time employment, I decided that we should do it ourselves. We wrote the book, obtained licenses, contracted with a graphic designer and printer, built an e-commerce Web site (www.actionsspeaklouderthanbs.com), established an LLC, and received "must buy" reviews from national media outlets and blogs including *The Nation* and the *Huffington Post.* Although *ASLTBS* never made the *New York Times* Bestseller List, the experience stands out because I recognized an opportunity, assessed and accepted the risk, executed the entire project on a tight budget and in a short time frame, and succeeded.

ANALYSIS

The author takes the reader through three events in his life, each exploiting an opportunity and leading to self-discovery. The essay is easy to read and conversational. The author is also able to articulate why these three achievements are important to him and what he has learned from these experiences. The essay demonstrates his continuous quest for growth, his crisp communication skills, and a determined attitude that is spiced with a sense of humor.

The first story gives a flavor of how the author deals with ups and downs in day-to-day life. He expected the internship to be glamorous and important but ends up stuffing envelopes in the office. However, the author is direct, accommodating, and persistent and eventually moves out of the basement into the limelight. The second story is probably the weakest—not in terms of content but in terms of explanation. The reader is not entirely clear as to what the author's role was in leading the team. Although the story gives an insight into the author's future ambitions, it doesn't help us understand his leadership style better. The author could have improved this section by enunciating "how" he was able to deliver "an innovative and compelling product." Addressing the "how" is more important than stating the achievement, and this section would be more convincing if the if the author had explained what he really meant by "leading a team." The final story demonstrates the author's fun-loving and risk-taking attitude. In terms of writing style, it is important to note how the author first simply states the achievement and then explains how he made it possible. The author is not afraid to reveal his lighter side, either—did he really expect to get on the *New York Times* BestSeller List? Probably not, but the story still remains memorable and makes us want to get to know the author more. Would he be an entertaining and eclectic contributor in the HBS classroom? Most likely.

ANONYMOUS

It was fall of my senior year, and I was attending one of the few financial services interviews I'd secured. The interviewer glanced at my resume, shoved it in a binder, and packed his belongings as he asked, "An English major—why aren't you going to be a teacher?" In 2002, the market for investment banking positions was bleak for Ivy League business students with strong on-campus recruiting. For me—a state school liberal arts major with few on-campus opportunities—there was no market, but I knew I could excel as an analyst. I submitted my resume online, applied to roles on-campus, but most importantly, I leveraged contacts. I diligently pursued a connection at a bulge bracket investment bank, obtained an interview, drove to New York for the final round, and received a full-time offer. I was proud, but when I arrived at training I realized just how competitive the pool had been. Most hires had been retained from the prior intern class. Over the next two years, I aggressively applied myself to succeed despite having no business background. Ultimately, I was a top performer, given a third-year offer. Securing the role and excelling demonstrated that with tenacious work ethic I could reach any goal. This achievement was pivotal for my career. It provided skills that would be crucial to attaining later positions in consulting and TechnoServe.

I love food. Chefs are my celebrities. I'm the go-to girl when planning any event, from corporate dinners to romantic celebrations.

The problem is, so many restaurants and—especially for me, a consultant—so little time. Although I was excelling at my consulting job, my hours were the highest in the firm. I enjoyed my career, but I needed to preserve my personal life. At the time, the French Culinary Institute was offering a food-writing class on Thursday evenings in New York. I was working in Connecticut. Attendance would require renting my own car and leaving the client site at 3:00 P.M. I made the case to my manager and he agreed. As a result, I improved my personal and professional life. The class itself was rewarding, and feeling fulfilled outside work allowed me to perform better on the job as well. I thought back to when I was twenty-two and a senior investment banker had told me, "You need to find balance." It took me three years to understand I needed balance to succeed personally and professionally.

I was alone in my room typing notes. I could have been anywhere, on any consulting engagement—except I was also hunched under a mosquito net in a dark, un-air-conditioned house with no electricity, feverishly finishing work before my laptop died. I was in Tanzania. A month earlier I was in New York. I was comfortable. I had a successful career and close friends. I wasn't passionate, however. My nonprofit involvement was marginal, and I wanted to test full-time development work. I lobbied my firm to take an unpaid sabbatical—something only one other consultant had done. I was nervous. The move stalled my career, and I wasn't sure my skills would have impact abroad. Nevertheless, it was the best move I've made. Professionally, my study was a success, has been distributed to eight countries, and will be presented at an international meeting. Personally, I had taken a risk by pulling myself away from my safe reality to test a possibility. Though it was a risk, there was a great reward: I was thoroughly energized about all aspects of my career, and I verified that I wanted a future career in economic development.

ANALYSIS

The author has provided us a classic example of someone who comes across as personable, real, and thoughtful. Her stories are simple and her story telling style is involving.

Some might say that enrolling in a food-writing class by itself is not a great achievement. What makes the story work, however, is how the author exposes her vulnerabilities and her strife to maintain a balance between her work and extracurricular life. As she has grown as an individual, so have pressures in her life, and she has recalibrated her priorities at each step in order to successfully manage those pressures.

The author chooses to arrange her accomplishments in chronological order. They don't have to be, but this works well for her because the themes show her thought process during her journey as an investment banker to sitting alone in a dark room in Tanzania charting her future path. The author has successfully beta-tested her interest in economic development via her sabbatical and convinces the reader that she knows what she wants.

Overall, the essay is successful because the author comes across as mature and balanced when she conveys what accomplishment means to her. Accomplishment for the author means understanding herself, overcoming setbacks, and logically charting out her future path. Do not fall into the trap of thinking that you have to come across as the next Jack Welch. It is great if you can differentiate yourself by your Herculean achievements, but it is more important to be original and engaging.

The message could have been even more effective if the author had found something other than chronology to bridge the three accomplishments. By focusing on how each accomplishment paved the path for the next achievement, the author would have added even more structure and flow to an otherwise solid essay.

Martin Brand

Four years after I had initially set myself the goal, I succeeded in winning the National Mathematics Competition in Germany. Seeing prolonged struggle turn into eventual success makes this one of my most valuable achievements. It helped me form an "it can be done" attitude that has stayed with me ever since. I first learned of the competition during a summer program in 1990 where I met some former finalists. The following year, when I was on exchange in the United States, I had the competition materials sent over from Germany. I made it though the first two rounds to become one of seventy finalists invited to a weekend where the five national winners would be chosen. I wasn't one of them. The following year I again advanced to the finals only to fail at the last test. I continued to work on my skills and when I made it to the finals for the third time in a row, I knew it was my last chance. I had to survive a grilling by university professors on an unknown topic, but this time I could solve every problem. Walking out of the interview I knew I had won. Three days later the letter arrived. It was a dream come true.

An accomplishment of a different kind is my work as an ambulance driver, which I chose as an alternative to military service. After gaining a qualification as a paramedic I started to man ambulances in my hometown near Düsseldorf. I worked both in supervised medical transports between hospitals and in emergency situations. My strongest memory is of the death of a child when we hit a traffic jam and could not make it to the hospital in time. I was in the back of the car with the boy and his mother. I never felt more helpless in my life. But there are also many happy memories, of the people whom we succeeded in helping during emergencies and of the many grateful patients on our regular transport services. During the fifteen months on the ambulances I matured tremendously. I learned to take on responsibility for other people when they needed me the most. I dealt with extreme pressure and human tragedy. These were enormous challenges to overcome, but every day I was also able to experience how gratifying helping others can be. I view my time on the ambulances as an achievement because I was able to learn and grow, but more importantly for the help we were able to provide to the patients and the community.

My third achievement is having a significant impact on the trading strategies of the currency options group at Goldman Sachs. I began developing my own pricing spreadsheets soon after I joined the group. Being in the privileged position of combining a strong mathematical background with the practical grasp of the market that our "rocket scientist" developers lacked, I was able to arrive at several innovations. While some enthusiastically supported my work (it would not have been possible otherwise), I encountered opposition from senior members of the group who lacked the younger traders' quantitative background and feared that eventually innovation would undermine their power base. I persevered, using my trading portfolio as a trial ground. Eventually, the better ideas prevailed and my interpolation now forms the basis of the strategy that group uses to identify value in the market. I am proud of having had the spirit and ability to innovate our strategies, but it is the strength to carry on in the face of adversity that makes this my biggest professional achievement to date.

ANALYSIS

Do not fall into the trap of thinking you have to come across as Hercules. It is great if you can, but such answers are neither realistic nor necessary. In the case of this essay, Martin shows maturity and humility by admitting his weaknesses and acknowledging how others helped him accomplish his goals. These traits make him humble and notable.

Martin describes how he handles adversity. Accomplishment for him is a process of overcoming failures and setbacks; his stories would not have the same impact if he had won the mathematics competition on the first try or had saved every person in his ambulance. He does not dwell on these setbacks, though, and instead focuses on how he overcame them. As a reader you are left remembering his "it can be done" attitude.

Martin chooses to arrange his accomplishments in chronological order. This works well because the themes of the first story resonate in the second and the third. Again, this level of coherence is not necessary, but adds to this essay's overall effectiveness.

ANONYMOUS

My three most substantial accomplishments have been genuine turning points in my life. Although they were emotionally trying and demanded a great deal of thought, sacrifice, and self-reflection, ultimately they strengthened my character and allowed me to better determine the life I want to pursue and the person I want to be.

The first of these accomplishments was my decision to return to Colombia two years ago. Even though I was working in a Boston consulting firm, had a tightly knit social network, and a loving, three-year boyfriend, I felt I was living the wrong life. Socially, I missed the diversity to which I was privy during college, and professionally I was not passionate about my work and did not find it satisfying. Leaving the United States would have been a simple choice had it not been for its heart-breaking implications.

Though profoundly enamored at the time, I needed to choose which was dearest to my heart and which was most important to my life: the country for which I was passionate or the person whom I loved; a promising professional life in Colombia or a fulfilling emotional life in the United States. The agonizing and painful weeks before and after my departure forced me to reflect upon the life I had, the life I wanted to lead, and the compromises I was willing to make for it. I concluded that my priority was having a significant impact in Colombia, and it became clear to me that only while doing so could I be happy.

The second of these accomplishments was my college triumph over a four-year eating disorder. I was acutely bulimic, and food determined my daily schedule; the routine was sickening and the grueling power of habit overwhelming. This shameful secret weighed upon my conscience, yet I felt reaching out was acknowledging weakness. I eventually overcame this apprehension and unloaded my burden onto my most trusted friends. With their help and my steadfast resolve I finally rid myself of the horrendous addiction. This is unquestionably one of the hardest battles I have fought and one of my most substantial accomplishments. I learned to ask others for help and I understood just how effective a team could be, even if the problem to solve was inside me. I also discovered I could rally a team and be a leader of change, even when I was the one in need.

My third most substantial accomplishment was summiting a 6,075-meter volcano in Peru. Beyond the physical and mental strain of the climb itself, this event was meaningful because I realized how averse I was to failure, how thirsty I was for success, and how far I would go to avoid one and attain the other. Despite my numb body and severe light-headedness, I reached the summit because I refused to admit defeat: I could not accept this mountain was beyond my capacity and could not bear to leave the challenge unfinished. I peaked with blind determination and effort, fully aware the risk of doing so was unjustified.

This experience was significant because it tested my willpower and gave me the courage and confidence to take on challenges beyond my comfort zone. It was noteworthy, too, because I recognized I had to be aware of my limits and be cautious when pushing myself past them. Finally, it taught me about my actions and the criteria that ought to guide them: if success involved risk, I needed to ascertain first if it was worth undertaking.

I consider these my three most substantial accomplishments. While my peers and parents would surely have suggested others, I chose them because they have been challenging, difficult, and thought provoking: landmarks on the path of self-discovery.

ANALYSIS

The first two achievmentments of this essay are remarkably fresh, candid, and self-exploratory. The author has chosen to focus on three mutually exclusive personal achievements rather than any career-related achievements.

The author subtly displays some of the essential characteristics of leadership through her three anecdotes. Through her first anecdote, she shows that she is clear-headed and capable of making tough decisions after careful deliberation. Through her second anecdote, she unlocks herself to expose her "shameful secret" and is not afraid to use graphic language to describe her bulimic life as "sickening." As a result, she comes out as a self-aware, courageous, and determined individual who is not afraid to ask for help. The final anecdote is a confirmation of a resilient young woman who will not give up until she achieves what she has set out to do. Her final anecdote, however, dampens the unconventional spirit of overall essay. After the build-up of the previous two anecdotes, it falls somewhat short in terms of originality and lessons learned. Note that we are not critiquing the accomplishment per se—climbing the mountain would have certainly been a challenge. The lessons learned, however, are not persuasive and unique enough to set this example apart from anyone else who may have climbed a mountain.

The author has proven that it is possible to display real accomplishments and demonstrate leadership in everyday life. The author is a doer. The essay is successful because the author has very effectively told the reader why these achievements are important to her personally. On the whole, these achievements tell a coherent story and help us paint a cohesive picture of what drives this person. It is important to reiterate that accomplishments in admission essays shine brighter with a meaningful and personal context and help the admissions committee learn what is important to you.

ANONYMOUS

My most substantial accomplishment is my success as finance manager at Helisur, in a position I took with no professional exposure to aviation, advanced degree, or managerial experience. My multiple responsibilities—managing relationships with financial and insurance companies, setting compensation policies, overseeing daily operations, collaborating with international suppliers—quickly outstripped my training as an industrial engineer. Lacking critical knowledge, I largely depended on self-education. I built a business book library, approached experts, attended courses, and spent countless nights building financial models. When first asked to provide a term sheet I looked up the definition on the Internet, gathered ideas from the books I had nearby, and delivered a proper term sheet by lunch without anybody noticing that I had no idea what a term sheet was earlier that morning. Clear goals and a healthy degree of confidence and optimism helped me develop essential business skills necessary to succeed in my position. By focusing on the critical strengths of our organization I optimized our financial management, established strong relationships with important local banks, and transformed our compensation system benefitting our employees and assuring top quality human capital for the company. By accepting the responsibility and meeting a tough professional challenge I made a positive difference for the organization and contributed to advance the project.

My second and very personal accomplishment was graduating first in a high school I started without knowing a single word of Spanish. The move from Russia to Peru changed my world. I lost contact with my childhood friends, my extended family, and my support base in the art school I attended for years and in the neighborhood I had lived in since birth. In Peru I discovered a completely alien environment and a challenge to fit into a new life. Pulled in many different directions and concerned about finding new friends and passing courses I barely understood, I discovered purpose in hard work and independence, learning to persevere in all my efforts. I set universally high personal standards, which I applied in everything I did, from choosing honest and down-to-earth friends to getting good grades. Five years later, the little kid from the former Soviet Union gave the valedictory speech, received three medals for distinguished achievements, including the gold medal for outstanding academic performance, and was applauded by his new friends and the entire community he finally called home.

My third accomplishment is having had a significant impact on my alma mater by co-creating an innovative Leadership and Management Control course. In college I discovered and pursued my passion for entrepreneurship in a variety of projects that were mostly independent and self-motivated because our industrial engineering program didn't have enough inspiring and practical resources to foster a culture of entrepreneurship. I collaborated with a friend and a young professor to design the first entrepreneurship course in the School of Engineering. Overcoming opposition of authorities who favored exclusively traditional coursework, we developed an innovative mixture of teamwork, leadership practice, project management theory, real-life cases, and guest speakers. My independent-learning managerial experience and success in team projects helped me prepare workshops and lectures designed to help students develop the strategic skills necessary to collaboratively identify, analyze, and capture opportunities. Using my passion for entrepreneurship, professional experience, and contacts as teaching resources, I contributed to make this course one of the most popular electives. I am proud of having had the ability and spirit to innovate and effectively contribute to my alma mater by solving a significant weakness in the program and improving the quality of education for future students.

ANALYSIS

In the first story, the author explains how he overcame a setback. He is a young and inexperienced kid who is underqualified but realistic. He openly acknowledges the gaps in his knowledge. How many times have you found yourself using the Internet search engine to look up something that others may find basic? We would think often. This section of the essay is effective because the author proves himself as a leader who is capable of learning, strategizing, and surviving when thrown in the deep end.

In contrast to the professional accomplishment described in the first anecdote, the author balances his essay with a more personal accomplishment—overcoming a language barrier—in the second story. His successful move from Russia to Peru is remarkable for any teenager. The cultural, linguistic, political, and structural diversity may have been demoralizing, but the author demonstrates his versatility, strength, and determination in successfully adapting to his new environment.

The third accomplishment again balances the overall thematic choices across the essay by focusing on an academic accomplishment.

We encourage applicants to balance themes across the three accomplishments to showcase their strengths via diversity of thought, expression, and experience.

The real shortcoming of this essay, however, is that the author does not delve into what he has learned and how he is a more capable person as a result of these accomplishments. The essay would have been more powerful if the author had elaborated on his thought process, including the "Three Ws": what drives him, why is the achievement important to him, and what has he learned as a result of these accomplishments.

Scott Griffin

1

Entrepreneur: In 1998, at the age of eighteen, I cofounded what is now Australia's largest online accounting firm—www.eTax.com.au. Together, my father, younger brother, and I launched an entirely new concept in the Australian market—"Do your tax return over the Internet." Since that time, several hundreds of thousands of Australians have registered to use our eTax product.

Under my leadership as business manager over eight years, we survived the dot-com bust—these were tough times, often working seven days a week around the clock. In 2001, I suggested and implemented an aggressive new marketing strategy that generated revenue growth of over 450 percent in that year. More recently, while simultaneously employed at the Boston Consulting Group (BCG), I launched a taxation call center in India that was the first of its kind for Australia. My brother and I developed all of the software including workflow management systems, online payments, and digital signatures. In 2005, we again doubled our revenues, and I am in the process of changing the way we think about our company structure and governance.

I feel it is a substantial accomplishment, first, to develop a successful national business and, second, to continue to do so while working full time for an international consulting firm, completing a triple degree, and touring the international music circuit.

2

Community leader: At present, I am leading a $10 million indigenous tourism project in Cape York, Australia. Indigenous Australians represent one of Australia's most disadvantaged minorities. The statistics are shocking for a first-world country—life expectancy at Mossman Gorge (where I currently work) is around fifty years of age. Nearby, wealthy "white" Australians have a life expectancy of seventy-seven.

Over the past four months, I have brought together a team of over twenty stakeholders including state, federal, and local government; national parks; community leaders; and investors. We recently agreed on a comprehensive plan to change the quality of life for residents at Mossman Gorge. Unable to find anyone else to continue this important work, I arranged project funding myself and have taken leave without pay from BCG to turn the plan into reality. Over the next six months, I will lead construction of an indigenous tourism business that will begin to transform this community from one dependent on passive welfare to one that is sustainable and self-sufficient. The project will be a role model for sixteen other disadvantaged communities in the Cape.

I feel honored, at a young age, to be given the responsibility and trust to run a multi-million-dollar community development project, and so far I am enjoying the challenge immensely.

3

International musician: for the past eight years I have sung as a tenor in over thirteen countries around the world, as well as across Australia. I sing with The Australian Voices (TAV), Australia's premier a capella ensemble, and performed with the Chamber Choir of the World in 2001.

One of many highlights was performing a harmonic overtone solo to a crowd of over seven thousand people in Llangollen, Wales, which was broadcast live by BBC television. Harmonic overtone singing is an ancient technique used by indigenous Australians for over forty thousand years when playing the didgeridoo. I have developed a skill using this technique to sing two notes at the same time, creating beautiful chords. As well as performing on the concert stage, I have given demonstrations of harmonic overtone singing to workshops of thousands of school children, teachers, and adult choristers across the world.

Personally, it gave me great joy to be recognized as achieving the highest professional artistic standards and to pass on my skills to my peers.

ANALYSIS

We chose this essay to highlight that there is no one defined formula or writing style that will lure the admissions committee. Scott is to the point and focused on facts, yet passionate about what he does. Scott takes a literal approach and offers three distinct bullet-point vignettes that do not necessarily bind together as a cohesive essay. It is okay to do so as long as the applicant clearly conveys his logic, not just the positive outcome.

Scott has chosen three achievements carefully, ones that offer a quick glance into his busy and interesting life that includes a capella performances, helping expand a family business, and leading an indigenous tourism business. Scott successfully demonstrates his sense of initiative, his leadership potential, his multitasking abilities, and his heterogeneous interests—admirable qualities in a business school applicant.

Scott tells it like it is. Nevertheless, the essay would have been stronger if he had been able to show rather than tell. You may have noticed that Scott chose not to dwell on his individual thought process. This distinctly contrasts with some of the other essays we chose for this book, which allow for more self-refection. This is probably the biggest critique of this essay. Although Scott's actions and positive outcome are abundantly clear, he undermines himself by dedicating only a few words to the takeaways from the experience. Furthermore, we still do not know what Scott would be like in a classroom. Scott has not revealed a lot about his personality and makes the following classic mistake: he has not reflected on how these achievements have shaped him. This essay would have been more effective if Scott had focused on *why* he chose these challenges and the lessons learned from these experiences.

Daniel Lewis

1

My most substantial accomplishment was my recovery from a motorcycle accident during my junior year at Tufts. On the way to Harvard Square, a drunk driver swerved in front of my oncoming motorcycle. My legs collided with the roof of her car, and I was catapulted through the air at over forty miles per hour, landing headfirst on the asphalt. I awoke from surgery eighteen hours later with four lacerated nerves and titanium rods securing my shattered femur, radius, ulna, and hand.

Following two weeks in the hospital, the orthopedic surgeon predicted I'd never have full use of my hand again, and suggested that I go to a special rehab clinic in California. "Rehab will fix my bones, but my brain will turn to mush," I thought. I phoned school the next day to find out which of my classes were wheelchair accessible. I spent the next semester wheeling through the Boston winter to physical therapy three times a day while studying astronomy and Russian.

It was the most painful, and challenging, time of my life. At graduation two years later, I was awarded Tufts's Ellen C. Myers Award for "outstanding scholarship in the face of adverse circumstances." The next day, I went back to Massachusetts General, and did four cartwheels across my doctor's office—never say never.

2

Next is the BroadbandCompass, a software program conceived in the basement of a nondescript building in a Denver-area business park. My five partners and I had only a dream, plus hand-me-down hardware and a few free ninety-day evaluation licenses for Web server software. We outlined the framework for our platform. Two years of strategy work at MediaOne Cable had convinced us it was time somebody made finding a broadband connection online as easy as finding a book on Amazon.com.

Funded with about a nickel over a million dollars, we labored for two years in that basement writing software code and convincing America's largest access providers, electronics retailers, and Web portals that our platform would change the way people looked for Internet access. We drudged through the Internet boom and the dot-com bust. But we made it. Today, our tool is leveraged by industry giants such as Office Depot, Microsoft, CompUSA, Circuit City, and numerous others. I am proud to say I wrote Product Specification V.1.0 for the technology that's helped one in ten Internet users find a broadband connection.

3

I am proud of my music. I have been obsessed with entertaining large crowds ever since I first laid hands on a pair of turntables in high school. I began my career as a bilingual "turntablist" my senior year abroad at a nightclub called Taxman in Moscow. Since then, I have developed a repertoire that includes gigs in some of Europe's and America's largest nightclubs, including sellout crowds of more than two thousand people. I enjoy convincing critics that mixing records is an art form, not just aimless basement shenanigans. Following the abrupt demise of a nightclub venture (see "failure" question for details), I founded Amazing Productions, Inc., a mobile disc jockey service. Though entertaining has never been my full-time occupation, it has always been my full-time passion. My knack for technology gives Amazing Productions a competitive advantage in the Denver market, as our shows have become known for their array of high-tech marvels. These range from blends of musical media—including vinyl, CDs, and MP3s—to computer-driven acoustics, lasers, and special effects. We have operated profitably and have become a household name in the Denver DJ industry. Check us out at www.amazingdj.com.

ANALYSIS

Daniel's essay is a winner because it is both substantive and stylish. He displays a dynamic personality not only through his achievements but also through his vibrant prose. His action-packed writing captivates the reader with colorful adjectives and striking descriptions.

Daniel is a memorable candidate because he is able to show rather than tell. His four cartwheels across his doctor's office display not only literary but also physical dexterity. He faces obstacles with humor and humility and paints himself as a fighter, not only through personal tragedy but also in the world of business. His diverse interests are captured with references to astronomy and Russian, programming and technology, and his passion for music. This essay stands out because the author comes across as an impressive personality and someone you want to get to know more deeply. That is a winning combination you may want to keep in mind when crafting your own text.

DALE SCHILLING

The Japanese language is highly complex. Two alphabets and a large number of kanji (characters) must be memorized, and respect for one's elders reflected in the grammar itself: to mistake this is to risk insult. At age seventeen, after five years of study at high school in Australia, I came to Japan with a few rudimentary phrases and four hundred kanji—the average Japanese high school student knows more than two thousand.

My move to Japan in April 1993 represented a great academic challenge—to attend lectures, research, and study under the same conditions as a native at a Japanese university—but also a personal opportunity, a tremendous chance to broaden my horizons. Five years in a foreign country and culture by myself was a daunting prospect, but I took the view that if I could not cope, I could always return to Australia fluent in Japanese after the one-year intensive language training course. The experience was both more challenging and rewarding than I had imagined.

The first year at Kyoto University was particularly tough academically. Although Japanese language school prepared me for the grammar and vocabulary needed, I was overwhelmed at first by the sheer amount of work required, taking two hours, for example, to read what took my Japanese classmates half an hour. Not only was I studying new concepts, but in a foreign language; a novel experience was to learn German and Chinese from a Japanese base. It was slow and painstaking work, but I refused to give up, setting myself arbitrary high standards. I used English books to study together with the Japanese texts, borrowed friends' notes to fill in the gaps I had missed in lectures, and with perseverance my language ability and grades improved.

At the university, a classmate asked me to join a newly established amateur musical drama group. I had performed in musicals and youth operas in Australia and was keen to join. We did everything ourselves, from creating the dialogue (in Japanese), music and dance routines, to backstage work (making costumes, sets, and lighting), to ticketing and marketing. The first performance had an audience of only one hundred in a crude yet intimate setting, but with time our productions increased in scale and hugely improved in quality. My strength is singing, and I am particularly proud that the vocal training regimens I implemented helped the group cope with the acoustics of the increasingly larger venues. I was also rapt when after one production I received a message addressed to the "foreign-looking detective" complimenting my performance. By my senior year, the group's performance was an established part of the Kyoto University Students' Festival, in a hall seating over one thousand people.

Upon graduation, I decided to work for a Japanese trading company. Many foreign students return home at that stage claiming some expertise in Japanese culture, but I realized I lacked the needed experience in Japanese business culture. I entered the company—only the second Westerner to do so—with much the same attitude that I had five years earlier: I have nothing to lose.

From the beginning I was treated no differently, expected to perform to the level of my peers. I appreciated and accepted the challenge, and I believe rose to it. Not only have I come to understand

Japanese customs—reporting techniques and the etiquette required in business discussions, for example—but also the Japanese way of thinking. This has not been to the detriment of my Western side, however. I believe I have maintained a global perspective and balance between cultures necessary for international business.

ANALYSIS

Rather than presenting three independent accomplishments, Dale writes a narrative of his decision to study and eventually work in Japan. While moving to a foreign country is probably not all that unusual in its own right, Dale sets the stage by explaining why Japan, in particular, was such a challenging place to live and study. From all three stories we learn that he is determined and persistent and willing to do whatever it takes to make the most of a daunting situation. While he concedes that he could easily have gone home if Japan did not work out, we come to see that Dale is someone who would never have given up until he had accomplished what he had set out to do.

The third accomplishment is perhaps the least compelling because while it reinforces that Dale approaches new situations with an open mind and a lot of determination, it does not say much about what he contributed to the organization. The essay would end on a stronger note if Dale had written about that rather than finishing with a somewhat confusing line about how living in Japan was not a "detriment" to his Australian heritage.

Erik Johnson

The three most substantial accomplishments in my life comprise an athletic, a personal, and a professional accomplishment. These have rewarded me with confidence in myself and my abilities, because they proved to me that I was capable of successfully handling difficult challenges.

The first accomplishment was the Pedro Zamora National College Bike Tour. I was one of five college students who organized, arranged financing for, and completed a cross-country bicycle tour from Los Angeles to Boston. We spoke at twenty-seven colleges with the objective of raising awareness on college campuses about the threat that HIV poses to college students. In Washington, D.C., we were received at the White House by First Lady Hillary Clinton. Additionally, we raised over $50,000 from corporate sponsors for HIV prevention education. I consider the tour to be one of my most rewarding accomplishments in terms of the physical and organizational challenges as well as the thought that we might have encouraged someone to behave differently and, thereby, potentially avoid contracting HIV. The trip also taught me how to push myself and my teammates to perform beyond our abilities as individuals.

The second accomplishment was living and working abroad for three and a half years. I knew that I wanted to travel the world and have a career in international business. I just did not know where to start or how to gain experience. I tried to obtain a job overseas while still in school but ran into the problem that I did not have any significant work experience. I almost decided to give up and wait until later in my career to work overseas, but something in my mind pushed me to take the risk and go for it. After graduating from college, I traveled in Australia and Africa for three months. When I ran low on money, I went to London in search of a job. Fortunately, I quickly found a job as an analyst for a firm based in Switzerland. I was soon transferred to the Swiss headquarters and then on to Chile. Over those three and a half years, I traveled to forty countries on six continents, gained significant international work experience, and learned a great deal about myself from exposure to new ideas and situations.

The third accomplishment results from a work experience. In June 1999, the company I worked for transferred me from Switzerland to Chile to conduct a survey of the Chilean market for a particular chemical used in the copper-refining process. If the market proved to be attractive, the company planned to construct a $2 million local production facility. My role was to develop a business model including market size and price structure, production costs, and a return on investment analysis to determine whether the plant would be successful or not.

I was somewhat daunted by the task, since a $2 million decision would be made based on my evaluation of the project. Over the course of six months, I met with the majority of our potential customers in order to produce a detailed market survey, found a suitable piece of property to locate the plant, worked with local engineering firms to develop plant construction costs, and produced a detailed production cost model based on market factors. After completing my analysis, I successfully recommended that the project not be pursued because of an unacceptably low return. This project offered me a significant level of responsibility, and I am pleased that I was able to meet such a tough professional challenge.

ANALYSIS

Erik comes across as courageous and curious, an individual you would want to sit next to on a long flight. Key to this is the tone of the essay, which is accessible, matter-of-fact, and not at all arrogant (always a risk when writing about things that you have done well).

He does a nice job by seamlessly moving from one story to the next. His colorful and detail-rich writing brings his accomplishments to life and results in a superb essay that goes beyond just saying something is good and instead proves it to you. As with many essays in this section, that is the key: convincing the reader that what you did is important to you, not that it is important in its own right. This may seem like a subtle point but it is worth remembering. Playing a tiny role in a $500 million deal but not having much to say other than that it was a big deal is a lot less meaningful than Erik's description of a relatively small project, but one where he had a major impact. Gaudy numbers matter less than what you did or what you learned. It is inevitable that someone else will have worked on a bigger deal, so try not to win based on size alone.

VI. SETBACK OR FAILURE

Describe a setback, disappointment, or occasion of failure that you have experienced. How did you manage the situation, and what did you learn from it?

Life would be dull if you got everything you wanted without having to struggle a bit. This question is all about how you deal with adversity. The key here is to turn whatever setback you experienced into something positive. Do not dwell on the disappointment—although describe it vividly—but rather focus on how you solved the problem and what you learned.

The following essays are terrific examples of individuals who did just that—they demonstrated initiative, adaptability, self-awareness, and strength of character in their reactions. These are stories both big and small. In choosing your own example, do not fret about finding a grand tale; this essay is about perceptiveness and introspection on your part, regardless of the scale of the event. You do not have to paint yourself as a phoenix rising dramatically from the ashes.

The failure essay is not trying to pick holes in your character; on the contrary, it is trying to build it up. Simply structured, it should step through the context, the setback, the consequences, the lessons, the solution, and the future application of your key takeaways.

We all have been beaten to the canvas, we have been dumped, we have flunked a test . . . and we should be thankful for it all. To fail is to have tried. The courage is in the ability to learn from your mistakes. This essay is your opportunity to show how you stepped back in the ring, found something new within yourself, and aced the test. In the words of the great British leader, Sir Winston Churchill, "Difficulties mastered are opportunities won." Show you believe that.

—Jamyn Edis

Chris Withers

A scaffold bolt had just whistled past my ear. It was my third day on a construction site and I had been assigned six men to complete the foundations. I was only twenty years old and lacked experience and confidence, which the men were exploiting. By the end of the week, another engineer had replaced me.

My first reaction was relief, but that was soon replaced by boredom with my new filing duties. I realized that my lack of training and experience had meant that I wasn't ready to manage a team. I met with the site manager and asked to shadow another engineer for the next two weeks to learn how to lead on a construction site.

I quickly learned the basic technical aspects of the role, but, more importantly, I recognized that the other engineers had a directive style, in contrast to my desire to lead by consensus. My problems had been largely caused by my leadership style, which had not been appropriate for the situation and which I had not adjusted appropriately.

After two weeks, I persuaded the site manager to give me another team. At the start of this role I adopted an authoritative manner, which was similar to that expected by the team of laborers. Once I had developed a working relationship of mutual respect with the team, I was able to relax some aspects of the direct management approach and build a rapport with the men.

This experience allowed me to practice different leadership styles and to understand the need to adapt my approach to suit the situation, the individual, and the team. I also learned about the role of confidence and credibility when leading a team, as well as the importance of training and mentoring for new starters.

ANALYSIS

In recounting the story of a setback in the workplace, Chris delivers a well-crafted narrative with pertinent lessons. With the detail of a bolt whistling past his head, the story kicks off with a punchy opener, providing both dynamism and humor. By the end of the first paragraph we know the context and also the setback Chris faces.

The story moves on quickly and Chris crisply frames a solution—the all-important element of a failure essay. He then drills deeper into the progress he makes, illustrating changed behaviors and maturity. What makes him stand out is his self-awareness, his ability to move swiftly, providing insight into his adaptive character. A smart move here is to tie in the evolution of his leadership style, which should be an important theme in all HBS essays.

This is a very strong essay. It is tightly structured, stylized, and presents lessons within an appropriate story line. Chris might have improved it slightly by removing some of the redundacy in the final two paragraphs and using the extra space to include concrete examples of how he applied the lessons outside the building site—whether in other work environments or in his personal life.

Eugenia Gibbons

My first project at Accenture consisted of an SAP implementation for Chile's largest copper mining company. Thanks to the experience I had acquired on the human resources module, I was asked to train the geographical division's personnel. I had spent several days preparing the training material and rehearsing before I arrived to the Chuquicamata site, the largest open-sky mine in the world, where forty administrative staff and supervisors were expecting me for weeklong training. They were all men and most of them former miners. The first session was terrible! I did not get any attention from my audience, and they were even disrespectful toward me.

There is a strong cultural rivalry between Chile and Argentina, to the point that some Chilean clients refuse to be served by Argentinean consulting teams. Additionally, very few women work in Chile, and even fewer are executives. That day, I had the feeling I was paying for both being an Argentinean and a woman. Nevertheless, I was extremely disappointed with my own performance and incapacity to control the group.

Toward the late afternoon, I interrupted the formal session and opened up the dialogue, reinforcing why I thought this training was important for all participants, and how it would affect their daily work. I also clearly stated how unprofessional their attitude had been and how it made me feel. After discussing what they wanted to get out of the training, we agreed on having eight extra hours to compensate for the time lost. From that moment on the group's attitude changed radically, my role was accepted, and the training turned out to be a great success.

What I learned from this episode was, above all, the absolute imperative to adapt the message and format of any presentation to its audience, and to identify and address the potential sources of conflict up front.

ANALYSIS

Eugenia finds herself in a tough spot. Many professionals will have encountered a similar situation—on unfamiliar ground, feeling underqualified, and facing a hostile client. Eugenia provides a great deal of detail in her story, and this helps the reader empathize with her situation as a woman facing cultural and sexist obstacles. With a limited word count you do not want to overinvest in setting the stage, but at the same time it is critical to take the time to tell a story people can relate to.

In describing her next steps, Eugenia walks through a three-point action plan and then assesses how she improved the situation. As in most good failure essays, the concluding outcome is positive. Eugenia demonstrates that she is able to react to setbacks in a mature and rational fashion, no matter how stressful the situation.

John Richard

One of my greatest struggles has been with my speech. I had a stuttering problem from age four that was a constant source of self-doubt until recently. In fourth grade, my parents took me to a speech pathologist in Houston who, through a yearlong program, "cured" my stuttering. After Exxon hired me, I experienced a demoralizing failure of speech that made me realize my stuttering was definitely not cured.

The cost engineering section had gathered to update our new worldwide manager on current projects and initiatives. We were supposed to introduce ourselves and summarize our activities. When it came time for my introduction, I turned toward him, reached out my hand in greeting, and said, "I'm J . . ." As I tried to say my name, my vocal cords locked. For what seemed like an eternity, I tried to force my way past the block, but the embarrassed stares from my peers and supervisors just increased my paralysis.

Eventually, I made it through the introduction and work summary but not before having that experience burned in my memory. Immediately after that incident, I started searching for a "miracle" drug to cure stuttering. After a few frustrating months, I realized that no cure existed so I purchased a self-help book. I practiced the exercises for several months and noticed some improvement in my speech, but when disfluencies still occurred, I felt helpless. After two more years of avoiding difficult speaking situations, I consulted the

Stuttering Foundation of America, which made me understand that stuttering is something that can never be completely cured but can be managed through self-awareness. To gain awareness of my stuttering, I have been keeping a daily journal of my speech habits. I document how my speech muscles react in stuttering situations and practice modifying or relaxing those muscles in similar situations. My newfound control over my speech has led me to actively seek out speaking situations that I avoided before. For instance, I was elected president of my homeowners' association, and I have shared several safety learnings in front of the sixty employees in my department. As my success grows, so, too, does my confidence to where I rarely experience speech blocks like I did at Exxon. I've realized that I must practice, practice, practice, however, and that I will be doing this the rest of my life.

While the concept of practice makes perfect isn't new, it has taken on new meaning for how I lead my life. I know that every aspect of my life where I'd like to see improvement must involve a substantial amount of practice, from negotiating skills to surfing, from networking with colleagues to training my dog.

ANALYSIS

John is brave to share a great personal challenge and his journey to conquer it. After a brief exposition of his stuttering problem, John dives right into the excruciating moment when he was confronted with an obstacle he thought he had overcome years ago. As a reader you empathize with him and want him to succeed. This essay, though, is not a tearjerker, and when writing your own essay you should be careful not to tell a sad story just to earn cheap points (because you will not). We feel his burning embarrassment, but we do not pity him.

John demonstrates his resolve by trying a self-help plan and seeking outside counsel. He then goes on to give real examples of how he applied these lessons and came to the realization that nothing will be solved without practice and hard work. Although this lesson may seem superficial at first, it captures the essence of a good failure essay—namely, finding the inner strength to surmount an obstacle, no matter how daunting.

Craig Ellis

Time never passes more slowly than when waiting for an actor to remember his next line. During my senior year in high school I earned the opportunity to direct a play, from casting to curtain call. What should have been a pleasant, two-and-a-half-hour performance, however, turned into a four-hour ordeal. I honestly felt sorry for the audience.

I did not realize the problems my casting had caused until two weeks before the show when the lead actress was suspended and the lead actor was still using cue cards he had hidden around the set. I should have mitigated my poor evaluation of my cast by replacing the lead actress and adapting my directing style to reap the talent of my lead actor. Instead, I continued with my plan, confident that my two actors would pull themselves together. The lead actress assured me she would be ready for the show, and the lead actor, who later went to Juilliard, would surely perform to his skill level.

My confidence was shattered that first long performance. My mistake was in my casting, but my failure was in my unwillingness to make the changes the play needed to succeed. This experience strengthened my skills in critically evaluating the strengths of my team members, but the lesson that has haunted me is that it is never too late to change direction when success demands it.

Years later, when I re-created the process-monitoring system at the Koch refinery, the first version was complete when I realized that major revisions were needed to keep the system running after I was gone; I had to change direction. I spent two months working extra hours to complete the revisions. Six months later, my assistance has not once been needed to maintain or operate the system.

ANALYSIS

You can almost feel Craig squirming in his seat as his actors bungle yet another line. But in this essay the writer does not miss a trick, delivering an offbeat example of personal disappointment. This essay is a good example of how you do not have to tell a story related to your job. In fact, lots of people do not. Do, though, remember to tie what you learned back to why you want to go to business school.

Here, Craig is conscious of telegraphing his key takeaways through a series of "shoulda, woulda, coulda" moments, showing how he wished he could have acted differently. This addresses the topic's requirement for personal learning, and makes the reader believe that the protagonist really did assimilate these lessons. In addition, the essay neatly dovetails into a second example, which illustrates the application of lessons learned to his project at the Koch refinery. This symmetry between the creative and commercial strands of the essay shows Craig as a well-rounded individual.

Irfhan Rawji

We had one thousand children and one hundred counselors on a cruise ship bound to Alaska. The project was the Young Presidents Organization family cruise, and I was contracted to help coordinate the youth activities under difficult constraints—space, time, and resources being the greatest of these.

To provide our clients with a memorable experience, we built a system that was capable of manipulating thousands of variables (staff, space, time, budget) into a solution that would allow each child maximum exposure to his or her favorite activity.

This solution was so complex that it confused the parents, children, and our staff alike. Extreme dissatisfaction emanated only three hours into our 168-hour contract. The project lead looked to me to uncover the source of our problem, as well as provide and implement the appropriate solution.

By hour twelve we had regrouped and redrawn our approach with a new understanding. Our objective was to ensure that each child went to bed with a smile; it was not to provide a custom adventure. Children were less worried about what they were doing than who they were with—fun, motivated counselors in an environment that included friends. We achieved tremendous success, resulting in accolades not only for our service delivery, but also for our flexibility and quick turnaround.

I learned that it is important to fully understand the client and her or his end objectives. Additionally, it is important to deliver a solution that is complex enough to meet those needs—but no more. We had spent too much time engineering the solution, and not enough understanding the problem. What seemed like a new and innovative approach was just a complicated, difficult, and time-consuming method of delivering fun.

ANALYSIS

Irfhan's essay is a good story about admitting a mistake and being willing to throw out lots of hard work and start over at a moment's notice. Irfhan fails to untangle the Gordian knot of his situation, but rather than admitting defeat, cuts through the problem with a simple approach. This shows creativity on his part as well as a lack of stubbornness. The result is that even though his initial plan did not work as he had hoped, he was able to save the day and prevent the cruise from being a total disaster.

The story is well-paced, delivering its central message within a structured framework: situation, complication, solution, takeaways. While you should feel free to experiment with the form your essay takes, with a limited word count you may not want to stray too far from this basic structure. One caveat: ending on a negative note can leave the reader with the impression that the failure was total and irreparable. In Irfhan's experience, this was not the case, and the final paragraph does illustrate the lessons learned. Nonetheless, unless you have a good reason not to do so, it is generally best to conclude with a positive accent.

THOMSON NGUY

I had just arrived in my unit, fresh from the U.S. Army Ranger School and the officer basic course, when my company set out on a twelve-mile foot march. By mile five, my radioman fell out of formation, unable to carry the extra weight of the radio along with the normal seventy pounds. Anxious to make a good impression, I eagerly took on his burden.

Around mile eight, I myself started running out of breath. I refused Sergeant Nelson's offer of help, determined to conquer this obstacle with tenacity, determination, and the stubborn refusal to give up. I marched for another two miles, hyperventilating each step of the way. Then, to my supreme embarrassment, I passed out. The platoon sauntered by me, their stricken platoon leader, as I lay along the side of the road while my sergeants doused canteen water on my groggy head.

I failed because of my pride. It was a lesson that would lead to a fundamental shift in my understanding of leadership. Instead of trying to be the hero of my platoon, I soon learned to accept the help of my sergeants. The ultimate success of the platoon depended on the actions of my squad and team leaders. The reserve of talent and potential there was far greater than anything I could have accomplished on my own. The best leaders, I learned, subsume their need for individual recognition in order to let their subordinates and superiors shine.

I changed my approach and our platoon excelled. Two months later, the battalion embarked on a twenty-five-mile foot march, a test of character and will. I marched at the head of the platoon, setting the example and encouraging the soldiers. My squad and team leaders kept their men in line, distributing the heavy equipment among themselves. Of the twenty-seven platoons in the battalion, ours was one of only two that finished without a soldier falling out. As for the radio, among myself, the radioman, Sergeant Nelson, Sergeant Gryder, and Sergeant Brown, we all shared the burden.

ANALYSIS

"Rangers lead the way!" is the motto of the U.S. Army Rangers. In this essay, Thomson demonstrates how he took this philosophy to an extreme, and as a consequence, failed those under his command. This story is great in highlighting the danger of hubris, and overcoming obstacles with energy, grit, and determination. It leaves the reader rooting for a successful outcome after a humiliating initial setback.

Fortunately for Thomson, he does not fall into the trap of assuming his idiosyncratic setting is enough to carry the essay. Instead, he shows an appreciation of learning through bitter experience. In this regard, he shows the applicability of a lesson across a spectrum of situations. As with the other successful failure essays, this story is dynamic, structured, and compelling, illustrating the evolution of an individual and a leader.

Anonymous

During my first consulting project, I was asked to construct a sales plan for an insurance company. The first step was to meet Adam, the director of sales, to discuss forecasting assumptions. A list of questions in hand, I knocked on the door. To my surprise, Adam was very formal in his reception. He did not understand why we were meeting, so I explained that I would be creating sales plans. At that point, he became outright hostile. He barked out his nonanswers to my questions and informed me he was very busy . . . preparing sales plans. Before I could suggest cooperation, I was ushered out, and the door slammed behind me. Too shocked to react to the secretary's condescending smirk, I attempted to grasp why a textbook opportunity for teamwork became such a spectacular failure. What had I done to attract such hostility? I had just wanted to help. I called my engagement manager to complain, but he just accused me of handling the situation poorly. I was crushed and convinced that I was not cut out for consulting.

To this day, I am not sure why Adam was so hostile. Retrospectively, I can only guess that he was insulted and threatened, because no one had formally requested his assistance. Instead, a twenty-two-year-old appeared in his office, ready to perform one of his most challenging tasks.

Adam and I never became friends, but the incident profoundly affected the way I communicate. Now, every time I interview a client,

I begin by exploring and allaying any fears the person might have. I explain the project's rationale and seek a frank reaction. The rapport thus established makes the interviewees comfortable enough to share private opinions. This very human interaction not only secures me with quick yet profound insights, but also relationships that often far outlast consulting projects.

ANALYSIS

This is a good failure essay in part because the main narrative does not have a happy ending. Many failure essays, in contrast, are really success stories told with a focus on the bumps along the road. In this case, the author is frank that he bungled his interaction with Adam. Although he does not say so directly, we can probably guess that he and Adam never had an especially productive working relationship (never mind that they did not become friends). As such, the essay is an example of a legitimate failure. When writing your own failure essay, do not waste time trying to sugarcoat a bad outcome. Say what happened and then move on.

The key, of course, is what the author learns from the experience. The answer: quite a lot. We see the author in a resilient light. He initially thinks he is not cut out for consulting but uses the experience to change his entire approach to interacting with clients. The result is a renewed focus on establishing relationships and building trust. The author has been humbled but emerges from the experience a more mature person and as someone skilled at working with senior-level executives. The ability to manage up in an organization as well as handle difficult conversations at all levels with both grace and candor will serve the author well at HBS and in his future career.

Jordan Burton

In the course of only a few months, my Bain colleague Graham and I transformed an idea into a company. We raised $1.8 million in venture funding, brought together a powerful and motivated board (including a former postmaster general and chief of staff under Lyndon Johnson), and hired nineteen incredibly talented individuals. We built the most feature-rich and user-friendly online address-change service available to the forty-four million annual U.S. movers.

By the late fall, revenues were growing nearly 50 percent month to month. This was not, however, sufficient to cover our cash burn rate. Though we had allocated resources with significant conservatism, we had always known that we would need an additional round of approximately $5 million to generate positive operating cash flows. In a series of frustrating setbacks, several strategic and venture capital investors pulled back their once overwhelming interest, leaving us with dissolution as our only option.

Despite our profound feelings of loss, Graham and I approached the wind down with the same degree of professionalism and courage as our initial fund-raising. We identified every stakeholder involved in our business, and made a joint decision that the welfare of our employees would come first and our personal financial considerations would come last. We leveraged our network of Atlanta business contacts to help each of our workers find jobs and arranged to sell the assets of the company to our business partner, Moving.com, for enough money to avoid bankruptcy and return some money to our preferred shareholders.

Despite the financial failure, the learning experience transcends the dollars and cents—Graham and I learned how to inspire a group of individuals to follow a vision and create something out of nothing. And we learned that, despite the risks and uncertainties we face, the only true mistake is to be afraid to make one.

Note: Certain identifying information has been changed to preserve confidentiality.

ANALYSIS

Jordan's story is a terrific illustration of what makes a successful failure essay. It demonstrates his individual drive, adaptability, and personal integrity. Furthermore, these characteristics are framed within a compelling narrative, striking a balance between its depth and being to the point. The text is tightly constructed with a beginning, middle, and end—a fundamental structural element of storytelling.

From the get-go, Jordan presents a scene that will be recognizable to many pre-MBA students. Jordan does not come across as a young hothead, expecting undeserved reward, but rather elicits sympathy as someone who cares deeply about the people who work for him and deeply regrets having let them down. Jordan is cognizant that his setback affects a great many constituents. Furthermore, he is concerned about his fiduciary duty to the stakeholders, placing himself at the end of the line for financial compensation. This shows tremendous maturity and leaves the reader with a sense that these characteristics will stick with Jordan throughout his career.

VII. ETHICAL ISSUES

In your career, you will have to deal with many ethical issues. What are likely to be the most challenging, and what is your plan for developing the competencies you will need to handle these issues effectively?

This topic represents a slight twist on traditional ethics questions that focus on a dilemma applicants have experienced firsthand: it is forward-looking, asking applicants to anticipate challenges they may encounter in the future as business leaders. Applicants may wish to use this opportunity to expand on their career goals or to address ethical issues that are specific to their chosen industry or job function. Despite the forward-looking nature of the question, students may wish to draw on past experiences handling difficult ethical dilemmas and demonstrate how this has shaped their principles as well as their plans for handling such issues in the future.

As with the other essay topics, simply relating a story is insufficient. Successful applicants also describe clearly what makes the anticipated issues so challenging. Successful applicants will also clearly answer the question's second component: What is your plan for developing the competencies you will need to handle these issues effectively? Applicants may wish to consider short-term and long-term plans, who will be involved, and why this plan will effectively prepare them for the specific challenges presented in the first half of the essay.

For many applicants, ethics may be extremely personal, and this topic provides a unique chance to share their personal views on ethics in a business context. While instinct is naturally a critical guide to action, it is important to note that people's instincts often differ and that few people have the ability to automatically identify all of the ethical issues involved in complex business contexts. While instincts and underlying principles should not be ignored, it is important to demonstrate your ability to identify, analyze, and resolve challenging ethical issues in a robust, structured fashion.

—Will Boland

Anonymous

I believe strongly that American industry needs to stay on American soil for our workers' sake and our economy's health. Our middle-class jobs, such as accounting and customer service, are being outsourced to India, and our lowest-paid jobs are going to imported labor. Even the "blue-collar aristocracy" of Detroit's UAW is facing uncertainty. International labor costs are making it difficult for American manufacturers to compete worldwide. Cheap, foreign labor is drawing American operations off-shore and Asian competition is intense. Meanwhile, unscrupulous domestic competitors substantially cut labor costs by hiring illegal aliens. American industry is facing an uphill battle.

As an American manufacturing leader in this climate I will face strategic decisions that have ethical implications and affect many people. Achieving economies of scale through growth and efficiency will minimize our competition's labor-cost advantages. Efforts to streamline and consolidate operations will force decisions on plant closings and capital investment. Such choices dramatically affect the lives of workers involved. When faced with the decision to shut down a plant, will I do so knowing it will cost hundreds of jobs? Perhaps we could improve the plant's profitability through capital investment, thereby saving jobs? Additionally: if maintaining the facility weakens our organization, doing so may cost many more jobs. Is it ethical *not* to close the plant? Facing these tough ethical choices will be difficult. Although I am confident in my personal ethics, as the head of an organization I will make decisions in situations that are currently foreign to me. Group pressures, accepted organizational norms, and powerful incentives will undoubtedly cloud ethical issues. In this context of incomplete and misleading information, it is naïve to think personal character, strength, and insight alone will let me recognize all moral questions and lead ethically.

Harvard's commitment to teaching business ethics is rare among American business schools. The core course Leadership and Corporate Accountability will prepare me in advance for inevitable ethical situations. The cases studied such as *Meinhard v. Salmon* and the civil protests on Royal Dutch/Shell's Nigerian operations are highly relevant to ethical discussions, and coverage of Stanley Milgram's chilling *Note on Human Behavior: Character and Situation* effectively highlights the need for ethical perspective. The case on Aaron Feuerstein's Massachusetts textile plant is particularly applicable to my situation. The Socratic case method will provide the defined situational experience necessary to help me navigate through ethical dilemmas in the future.

ANALYSIS

The author makes a strong statement on a fairly explosive issue in today's business world. In doing so, he delivers a strong personal message: he is not afraid to take a stand on a sensitive issue.

The key to the essay lies in the second paragraph, where the author poses a series of dilemmas he expects to encounter as a U.S. manufacturing executive. In leaving these questions open-ended, he softens the somewhat rigid image presented in the opening paragraph. He does not purport to know the answers today, only that these questions will likely be highly relevant to a future career in U.S. manufacturing. In a sense, the author transforms throughout the essay, recognizing that solutions to these challenges will not be self-evident and that he must work hard to develop the competencies necessary to address these challenges in the future. Asking many questions models a solid, transparent approach to problem-solving that will ensure he considers multiple perspectives to inform his decision. Furthermore, the author does an effective job of highlighting that incomplete information and certain pressures may cloud his personal judgment, making reliance on personal values and instinct an incomplete approach to analyzing ethical challenges in the future.

The author could have improved the essay by elaborating on his development plan, integrating additional plans into the final paragraph as opposed to focusing strictly on the resources available at HBS. All in all, the strength of this essay lies in the fact that the applicant masterfully conveys that he is likely to be someone who will not be afraid to engage in productive debate and challenge his classmates and coworkers.

PAUL YEH

The automotive industry is under duress. Company executives are cutting healthcare benefits, freezing pensions, and laying off workers. While corporations have responsibilities toward their stakeholders, how does an executive balance between his employees and shareholders? As I continue my career in the automotive business, I will undoubtedly face the ethical issues of balancing between profits and people.

During the Explorer launch, I experienced one such issue. On the chassis assembly line, Ted, an operator, complained that his hands were becoming numb from trying to insert a part. The engineer's solution was to revise the attachment, but it would cost $70,000 to retool the part. Typically, the finance department would reject the issue because the measured insertion effort was within the UAW contract. But contract or no, it seemed wrong to cause an employee to damage himself. So, I tried Ted's job for thirty minutes. I picked up the part, walked six feet toward the assembly line, and pushed the part into the frame. The first dozen were effortless. I noticed, however, that the repetitive motion strained the wrist. I wanted to fix the issue, but approving an expensive change when Ford is not liable is a hard sell to management. Rather than approving or rejecting the costly solution outright, I brainstormed with the engineer and explored alternatives. Two days later, we came up with a cost-efficient way of lubricating the attachment for easier insertion.

The material costs less than $20,000, and I convinced the finance management to accept. Ted was extremely appreciative: he gave me a bear hug.

To continue developing my competencies, I will observe how Rick Wagoner, Lee Iacocca, and other executives balance profitability with employees. I will then discuss their rationales with renowned professors such as Malcolm Salter, who has done extensive research in the automotive industry. Harvard professors will help me understand each situation's intricacies and in turn cultivate my decision-making process.

Additionally, I will continue to interact with Detroit Executive Service Corps volunteers, most of whom are retired automotive executives. Similar to Harvard's Leadership and Values Initiative Speaker Series, I will learn from these leaders' experiences and see what competencies have been practiced, and which have worked and which have not.

Finally, I will continue to go to the front line so I can assess each issue effectively. Then, armed with the academic training and practices from courses such as The Moral Leader, I am confident that I will be able to approach and resolve challenging ethical issues.

ANALYSIS

Much of Paul's success lies in his ability to clearly address each component of the question presented. He clearly describes the challenges he anticipates, offers a compelling ethical dilemma that helped shape this view, and spends roughly one-third of his essay describing his development plan. Throughout the essay, Paul keeps his discussion grounded in specifics related to his prior experiences and future goals rather than offering generic philosophies. Furthermore, by weaving in personal anecdotes such as jumping onto the line and receiving a bear hug from the line worker, Paul adds life to the page, engenders credibility, and reveals new elements of his personality such as his determination, persistence, and empathy.

This essay also provides an example of someone clearly capable of identifying, analyzing, and resolving an ethical issue in the face of significant political obstacles. Paul not only identifies an ethical dilemma but also considers thoroughly the implications and consequences of different plans of action. Given the limited liability and cost-containment pressures facing his employer, Paul knows that a simple argument of the principles and an expensive retooling effort are not likely to be successful. Recognizing this obstacle, Paul engages his colleagues to devise a more pragmatic solution that was able to survive a bureaucratic review due to its lower cost. By developing a clear understanding of the problem, brainstorming various solutions, and analyzing likely consequences, Paul dramatically improves his chances of achieving his goals. Altogether, Paul's essay paints a picture of a likeable, dynamic, and pragmatic individual with significant initiative and leadership ability. Moreover, Paul demonstrates that a specific, in-depth example can powerfully convey an applicant's leadership style and personal ethical framework for approaching controversial issues.

Rye Barcott

Marines learn thirteen leadership traits at boot camp. I stress two—integrity and loyalty—during initial counseling sessions with junior Marines. These two qualities are my expectations. Integrity means they will be honest with themselves and me. Loyalty entails faithfulness to the organization, and their seniors, peers, and subordinates. The most challenging ethical issues I am likely to face are those that arise at the juncture of integrity and loyalty. How, for example, should I handle a situation in which a supervisor, peer, or subordinate I admire compromises his or her integrity?

My upbringing blessed me with a strong moral compass, but knowing "right" and "wrong" is insufficient for handling ethical issues with complex, unpredictable repercussions. The best preparation for ethical challenges is to study historical cases and reflect on one's own experience. I'm seeking opportunities for the former, which is one reason I'm applying to business school. Nevertheless, I've learned from my own experience. One event's impact was particularly profound.

John, an orphan who excelled at soccer, became Carolina For Kibera's (CFK) youth coordinator in 2001. He was responsible for the CFK sports association and its two thousand members. Wanting to advance his education, John took the SAT and scored a 1,090. I helped him assemble undergraduate applications and secured funding from two of CFK's most committed donors. John was accepted to

UNC-Chapel Hill. It wasn't until the U.S. Embassy scrutinized his records that we learned his transcript had been fabricated.

Although John compromised his integrity, I felt loyalty to him as his supervisor and friend. I considered allowing John to return to CFK. I consulted our Kenyan leadership. We discussed the impact on other Kibera youth aspiring to attain a college education. John's loss was not only his; it was the organization's. It affected not only an individual but a community—how we handled it would define CFK's ethos.

We decided to remove John from CFK and reevaluated the core values of our organization, eventually creating a Fair Play Code. I called the donors and explained what happened. We responded appropriately, but my enthusiasm for John to succeed had encouraged his actions. His case reinforces the responsibility of leaders to establish and maintain standards of integrity and loyalty, and John is always in the back of my mind when I conduct initial counseling sessions with junior Marines.

ANALYSIS

This essay stands out for the way the author instantly engages the reader with an interesting ethical juxtaposition and later reveals his personal struggle to find compromise when two of his most important values—loyalty and integrity—end up at odds. Rye's first paragraph is effective because it quickly and clearly conveys this issue. The subsequent example is compelling in and of itself, but more importantly, it helps the reader further understand the scope of the dilemma and why Rye considers it to be so challenging.

Rye seems to have grown so close to his mentee that he did not want to believe this failure of integrity, a subtle element of the story that gives the reader a sense of the powerful emotions racing through the author's mind. After considering the implications on others in the organization, Rye decided to prioritize integrity over loyalty, coming full circle with the juxtaposition posed earlier in the essay. In doing so, he shows a deep awareness of the consequences of his decision on the broader mission of his organization. Despite the loyalty he feels toward his mentee, Rye conveys an ability to step back and analyze his alternatives rationally and objectively. He thereby demonstrates immense personal maturity by distancing himself from his emotions while considering the long-term implications of his actions.

Toward the end of the essay, Rye wavers a bit. The uneasy tone indicates that he may not be entirely certain that he made the right decision. In the realm of ethics, reasonable people will disagree, and errors will be made. If there is anything that Rye could have done to improve his essay, however, it would be to provide a more detailed evaluation of the pros and cons of giving John another chance versus using him as an example for others at CFK. Either way, the essay leaves the reader with the impression that Rye is a strong mentor and friend but also an effective leader who recognizes the impact his decisions have on those around him.

Anonymous

In aviation, safety is paramount. It requires proven pilots, capable maintenance, efficient logistics, quality spare parts, and administrative policies that promote the right attitudes. Management must have a solid moral conviction to not take shortcuts while making every effort to improve operational safety for the company, its employees, and its clients. Every decision counts. Choosing a cheaper but unproven component supplier may amount to an ethical challenge because without proper evaluation it can compromise the whole operation. Unhappy mechanics or distraught pilots are a risk no aviation company can afford. The unstable economic and regulatory environment in Latin America combined with the unfair competition from the armed forces in the past drove many private aviation companies out of business. The survivors had to adapt and take shortcuts that probably contributed to the region's mediocre safety record.

When I arrived at my first job, the situation was no different. Local companies paid their flight crews by the hour flown or day worked. Lack of civil aviation schools meant that new hires came from the armed forces, where extremely low wages made recruits very eager to accept employment in the private sector. As a newcomer to the industry, I perceived that this compensation model created a perverse incentive for pilots to take unnecessary risks to earn the extra hour. It was a choice between a cost-saving practice and our vision of safe operations for which the practice was a liability. Convinced that our resource allocation had to follow our vision, I developed and implemented a performance-based compensation system, ensuring a stable monthly income with full benefits for our pilots. I supported the initiative that significantly increased our labor costs because it contributed to improved safety, the critical factor for our operations.

In aviation, compensation policies, working conditions, supplier choices, and investments in optional equipment or nonessential training all have strong ethical implications because of their potential side effects. To succeed I will have to invariably keep people and safety first, stay true to my vision, and exhaustively study every optimization initiative or cost-saving measure to ensure full understanding of its impact. The HBS case method with its multiple perspectives and conflicting priorities, combined with exposure to challenging decision-making scenarios and business leaders and organizations that succeeded in comparable situations, will help me strengthen my ability to focus on vital priorities and make optimal decisions based on a comprehensive evaluation of their impact on my venture's critical success factors.

ANALYSIS

The author of this essay addresses the difficulty of staying true to his values in a region where competitive dynamics and an uncertain regulatory environment have led the industry to adopt certain practices that are inconsistent with the applicant's beliefs. He paints a vivid picture of the dilemma, providing specific details that make the story plausible and shows his thought process as it applies to the complex ethical challenge.

As the applicant clearly explains to the reader, adopting stringent safety measures—something the author views as a basic duty of industry managers—is not an explicit requirement in the market where his company operates. Following the industry norm, despite its negative impact on safety, would not merit criticism or blame. Nevertheless, the applicant explains that not taking action would violate his "vision" or deeply held belief that his company has an ethical responsibility to take action. In many business situations, industry norms may not be consistent with a manager's personal principles, and difficult decisions must be made. By adopting a high safety standard when industry standards dictate otherwise, this applicant demonstrates that his deep conviction and integrity guide him effectively when facing such dilemmas. The applicant's careful analysis also demonstrates his maturity and objectivity by exploring the trade-offs his actions might entail between the company's competitiveness/performance and collateral stakeholders, including customers, suppliers, and employees.

One mild criticism of this essay is the unnecessarily long and convoluted final sentence. Tying HBS into a development plan can be effective but is certainly not necessary. Here, the author's development plan becomes unclear and distracts from an otherwise strong essay.

Adam Heltzer

Infrastructure projects in low- and middle-income countries are rarely an unqualified boon to the economy, free of negative externalities. The land used to build a power plant for an underserved segment of the population may displace another indigenous community. Efficiency improvements in a metropolitan water system may also raise the price of water for families that can barely afford to eat. Throughout my career, the decision of whether to invest in such projects will have to weigh what sacrifices should be made for the "greater good."

As if this were not a significant enough challenge, it is likely that I will often be dealing with imperfect and contradictory information from fractionalized governments, poorly translated information, and stakeholders who have less than altruistic motives. While developing a cookie-cutter response to such complex moral dilemmas is inadequate, I can rely on some guiding principles learned from previous successes, failures, and mixed outcomes in challenging ethical situations.

First, I've learned the value of thoroughly evaluating the alternatives and potential compromises between two sides, rather than opting for an adversarial zero-sum decision. In the case of one Brazilian wastewater treatment project, I helped design a public-private partnership that spread the risks and rewards of the project between the state government and the private operator, utilizing the strengths of each. Carefully crafting an arrangement in which both sides can "win" if they collaborate has created a healthier environment for implementing the project.

Also, when weighing a difficult decision, I always try to separate passion for the immediate outcome from the broader consequences of a decision. This was the case when I implemented fundamental changes to my fraternity as president in order to curtail behavior that was detrimental to the organization. Though I knew the changes would cause some members to deactivate, I was willing to make that sacrifice for the long-term health of the fraternity.

Underlying these experiences, my Jewish upbringing has formalized a continuous process of ethical introspection, a sort of constant moral compass that has always helped me retain perspective when grappling with overwhelming and ethically challenging situations.

I'm looking forward to testing my guiding principles in the case environment at HBS, where the LEAD courses will play a key role in sharpening my ability to handle ambiguous ethical situations. Simulating difficult managerial decisions with classmates of widely varying backgrounds will help me learn how to assess information, weigh options quickly and effectively, and mitigate negative effects.

ANALYSIS

Adam's essay is successful because it is well-structured and revealing. Adam has clearly thought through the most important ethical dilemmas he is likely to face, given his desired career path, and subsequently offers two supporting anecdotes that provide insight into his personal values and how these have been tested in different formats. Importantly, he does not leave the reader on the purely theoretical plane laid out in the first two paragraphs. Adam provides the reader supporting vignettes—one from the workplace that had implications on his career and one from his personal life where friendships were at stake. These stories demonstrate to the reader how his moral code manifests itself on a practical level. Furthermore, Adam effectively uses each to demonstrate his ability to make difficult decisions when his career or personal responsibilities have been at odds with his ethical stance. On the other hand, these stories would have benefited immensely from additional detail such as shedding light on the contradictory emotions he likely faced during his attempt to find an ethically agreeable solution.

In relating personal stories, applicants should be certain to clearly highlight the situation's core conflict. What made (or, if forward-looking, what will make) the ethical dilemmas such a profound test for you? In addition, while the focus of this essay topic is your future career, it is important to note that ethical dilemmas arise in many contexts, as Adam's essay demonstrates. If a personal situation has profoundly shaped or tested your ethical stance, you should not shy away from sharing this with the admissions committee. Furthermore, in reflecting on your development plan, try not to focus exclusively on Harvard Business School. Consider your family, friends, mentors, industry leaders, daily practices, or other means that you believe will make you more adept at handling ethical dilemmas in the future. Incorporating HBS into your development plan is effective only if you directly tie the experience into the development needs discussed in your essay.

Anonymous

It is the year 2015. I am sitting in my office in Mumbai, India, where I am working as the regional manager of an international consumer goods company. I am brand manager for the country's most popular soap. The objective of this brand is twofold. The company is running a profitable business and through their business contributing to public health. By washing their hands with our soap, over a million children are saved from death caused by diarrhea-related diseases every year. Pearls of sweat manifest on my forehead due to the tropical heat and the difficult decision I am facing.

Just now I learned that our soap has unexpected negative environmental consequences because it is polluting the drinking water, resulting in a threat to public health. The twofold mission of profits and public health has turned into a paradox. On the one hand, if we pull back our soap from the stores, people will get ill if they cannot wash their hands with soap and our profit will go down the drain. On the other hand, if we keep selling the soap, people will get ill from drinking polluted water. What I will need in this challenging situation is to first create transparency by estimating the actual size of the issue. During my third year at McKinsey I expect to refine these skills. Second, I will have to make a judgment call based on my personal values of justice and social responsibility. My personal values, which also guide me in my professional role, are largely established and will continue to grow in time. Third, at Harvard Business

School I hope to further develop the skills to take decisions and to convince others of them. These skills will facilitate me when communicating my decisions and delegating tasks, enabling me to focus on a long-term plan. Fourth, at HBS it is my aim to evolve the long-term planning skills that I have gained through my strategy experience. Finally, interaction with fellow students and professors who are bound to have different views on ethical issues will allow me to understand my ethical standards in the light of theirs. Moreover, visiting the classes on Corporate Citizenship and (at the Kennedy School of Government) Public-Private Partnerships, I realized that through the Harvard MBA program I would develop meaningful mentor relations. The mentorships that I have established at McKinsey have proven to be invaluable when facing challenging issues.

ANALYSIS

The author's purely forward-looking approach and vivid storytelling set this essay apart from the pack. In contrast to a majority of essays that reference past experiences and extrapolate more generally toward the future, the author of this essay chose to craft a specific example of a difficult ethical challenge she may face in the future as a consumer goods executive. Though this purely forward-looking, fabricated example is risky, the author captivates the reader with vivid imagery. Anxiety seems to bleed from the page as the reader envisions the author facing the dilemma as "pearls of sweat manifest" on her forehead. The author balances her futuristic story with a pragmatic, step-by-step outline of the skills and resources she must develop to appropriately respond to this dilemma. From her third point on, however, the author weakens her essay by straying from her forward-looking approach and wandering into a discussion of development needs, mentors, and the HBS experience. The author could have improved this essay significantly by more clearly tying her development plan into the ethical dilemma concept. The author could have further improved this essay by sharing more explicit insight into her personal values. While the author tells an interesting story, describes why this challenge would be so difficult, and demonstrates an ability to think carefully through the issues at stake, she somewhat hides herself behind the story. Ethics can be extremely personal, and applicants should not be afraid to shed light on their fundamental beliefs.

Anonymous

In my experience thus far, it has been situations where the logical and moral evaluations diverge that have proven to be the most challenging ethical issues for me to resolve, and they will likely remain so. In trying to use a similar approach to tackling each of two very different dilemmas, I learned that I needed to develop more flexibility. In fact, the combination of these two experiences has led me to identify the key to this flexibility: effective evaluation comes from the interplay, rather than the choice, between logic and morality.

While interning at a consulting firm that had recently made headlines for biased, unethical recommendations to clients, my boss asked me to change my fact-based analysis to arrive at a safer, more client-friendly conclusion. But my analysis was very clear; in this case there was a right answer and a wrong one, and he was advocating the wrong one. I let the facts drive my argument and reapproached my boss. At the end of the day, I allowed the fact-based accuracy of my work to convince him to change his approach.

In a different instance, I would rely on my morals to derive my answer. While between projects at McKinsey, I came upon a great opportunity. The clients were thoughtful and appreciative of consultants, the hours flexible, and the team top-notch. We were also hired to tackle a thoroughly interesting problem. The work, however, was for a tobacco company. After years of discouraging friends and loved ones to stop smoking, the task felt tantamount to asking me to sell cigarettes. I could not quiet my conscience. At the same time, logic pointed me toward the project, since the firm would find others to do it if I wouldn't, and my other options were limited. The more I tried to use logic to derive an answer—my default approach to problem-solving—the more I realized that the logical answer wasn't my answer this time. I could not and would not work for the tobacco company. I turned the project down.

In the past, objective logic had been my default evaluative criteria, but this experience taught me to value my own moral code as well. Now, it is through a constantly evolving interplay between logic and morality that I look to answer ethical questions. I do not intend to go to business school to develop a perfect formula for addressing ethical dilemmas. Instead, through continued exposure to complex ethical questions, I will develop deeper competencies and more finely tuned instincts, so that I can more consistently choose the "right" path.

ANALYSIS

The author of this essay sets himself apart by detailing the extent of his self-exploration effort. Through his experiences, he has learned that ethical dilemmas are rarely black and white. Instead, they require a delicate balance and interplay between his logical business judgment on the one hand and his sometimes conflicting personal moral code on the other. This essay topic presents candidates with another opportunity to share the experiences, personal and professional, that have shaped their values, as well as to demonstrate their potential as business managers. This writer does both effectively.

Neither naïve nor cynical, he is aware that ethical dilemmas will arise and strives to confront them using his deeply held beliefs. He provides two detailed examples from his career, one supporting his business logic and one supporting his ethical code, to illustrate clearly how his view on the interplay between logic and ethics has been tested and developed. He makes it easy for the reader to visualize these experiences through his straightforward and illustrative writing style. At the same time, the author uses these experiences to cleverly paint a picture of himself as an effective and dynamic leader. Through his thoughtful reflection and resolution of the dilemmas he describes, the author demonstrates pragmatic business strengths: flexibility, problem-solving, and communication skills. Furthermore, his maturity and forethought are conveyed in his awareness of how this conflict will affect him in the future. It will require continuous development and daily resolution as he deals with more important issues while progressing in his career.

VIII. OTHER QUESTION

What other information do you believe would be helpful to the Board in understanding you better and in considering your application?

What an interesting topic! Open-ended questions are challenging because candidates have to go through the sometimes harrowing process of deciding what to talk about. They can, however, be the decisive, positive factor in an application. We encourage applicants to think of this question as an opportunity to display elements of their personality that haven't come across in their other essays. For example, some applicants choose to talk about their family life and their personal values; others touch upon specific aspects of their personalities that they think will differentiate them from the rest of the applicant pool. What's important to know is that there is no best answer, no best approach, no best topic, but it is essential that the message remains consistent with previous essays submitted by the applicant. While maintaining that consistency, successful essays in this category fall into two broad groups: on the one hand, the ones that reinforce the candidate's previous analysis, thoughts, and observations about themselves, and on the other hand, the ones that mark a sharp contrast with the previous essays in an effort to demonstrate a multifaceted personality and an ability to approach problems from various angles. Both approaches work, providing they convey a clear message.

As for the tone of this essay, candidates have absolute freedom as to how to best express themselves. Serious or light, again the important thing is that tone and topic treated are appropriate and logical. For example, if you choose to talk about how your first entrepreneurial venture was selling ice cream in minus-ten-degree weather, it's perfectly appropriate to adopt a humorous tone while invariably demonstrating your salesmanship.

The following essays span a variety of those choices. They represent the last touch of the painting, the final "taste" that applicant leaves with the reader. Let that reader into your mind. Be creative. Be humorous. Be open!

—Linda Dempah

Nathan Dutzmann

A quick proofread of the other five essays suggests that they don't entirely capture me. Allow me to introduce myself.

Truth be told, I'm not necessarily the easiest person to get to know well. The ingrained risk aversion to which I alluded in Essay Two often tries to manifest itself as inconspicuousness in social settings. I realized many years ago, however, that I could either cave in to my shyness or I could mask it and overcome it with a cloak of humor. To the latter end, I have worked to develop my wit. My style of humor ranges from goofy gregariousness to a withering deadpan that at times totters precariously on the edge of irreverence. In joking with my Australian coworker that his is a nation justifiably proud of the convictions of its forefathers, I need to be *really* certain that he'll take it in the right spirit. Still, humor has helped me to become successful in social settings. When the rare friend who gains my trust sufficiently for me to reveal my inner shyness responds with, "But you seem like such an outgoing and funny guy," I'm very glad I didn't cave.

Perhaps paradoxically, I love public speaking, though I don't have the opportunity as often as I would like. Speaking in front of many unknown faces is less daunting than meeting one new person. Humor helps here as well. I even have coworkers who prejudge our firm's quarterly meetings by a binary boredom index that hinges on whether I'm scheduled to give one of my not-so-standard presentations.

I play basketball, ultimate Frisbee, and the fiddle, each but recreationally and all with less skill than I could wish. My greatest passion is knowledge. The stack of eight books that is currently sitting under my bed, all of which I will finish, reveals my primary means of satiating that passion. I also love creative writing. My long-suffering friends periodically receive whimsical essays on topics like the horrors of driving in New Jersey or the improvement of love songs by replacing "you" with "food" ("I love food truly, truly dear . . ."). I'm also slowly writing a complete commentary on the Bible, but my muse is short-winded, so I am thankful to the nameless medieval monk who divided the scriptural tome into convenient, bite-sized chapters. For this reason I am also thankful to the HBS Admissions Board, to wit: 398, 399, 400.

ANALYSIS

This applicant conveys two main ideas in this well-structured essay. First of all, he chooses to focus on his style of humor and demonstrates it by keeping the actual tone of his essay light and witty. At the same time, he also shows that he has a sound understanding of himself and is aware of how he best relates to others.

The introduction immediately draws the readers into the story with a witty, memorable, and somewhat direct intro: "Allow me to introduce myself." He entertains his audience, opens up without boasting, and puts his sense of humor on display. The candidate achieves that outcome by presenting a thoughtful, well-crafted argument in which he touches upon the interesting paradoxes of his personality. He is shy, yet enjoys public speaking; he is humorous, but cautious with his levity, so as not to offend his interlocutors.

Other Question

This essay is masterful because it is unique and gives the audience insight into the writer's personality. The last paragraph shows that he is a fun person who uses humor to break social barriers and entertain his "long-suffering" friends. In the last sentence of the essay, the candidate proves that he has an original ability to improvise and think on his feet. "To wit: 398, 399, 400." On the basis of personality alone, this author has distinguished himself, which is exactly the intended outcome of this wide-open essay topic.

Anonymous

While I share what I have done and hope to achieve, my story is incomplete without explaining the "why." Alone and with no resources, my mother fled the religious persecution of the Baha'is in Iran to ensure the safety and education of her four children. Like other immigrant families, ours struggled to meet basic needs. Nevertheless, inspired by my mother's sacrifices and commitment to education, we have emerged from our initial poverty as professionals. I seek admission to Harvard Business School because of an urge to honor the opportunities that both U.S. asylum and my family made possible.

Not only is a college education a mere fantasy for a member of the Baha'i faith living in Iran, but also ambitions of female business leadership likely would be limited to a dream. My mother and sisters instilled in me the significance of rights and freedoms that were unique to both Baha'is and to women in America. Not only did my single mother head a household, but my sisters competed in the field of electrical engineering. Growing up watching my siblings juggle multiple jobs and full-time schoolwork to contribute to our survival instilled in me lessons of discipline, sacrifice, and hard work. I, too, financed my college career, except with scholarships that enabled me to devote my extracurricular time to service. I strove for academic excellence and contributed to helping others just as my siblings provided for my family. I pursue an HBS experience to make my future service more efficient and effective.

When asked where I am from, I respond with an introduction to my family and faith to help the inquirer understand me far better than any declared country or culture. I live by a motto that my work is a form of worship. The wealth I wish for is not limited to that which is measured with dollar signs. Rather, I hope for my wealth to be measured in knowledge acquired, and my success measured in knowledge applied as a servant who enables others to reach their goals. I have raised funds, built a school, and opened a clinic around the world by enlisting the participation and resources that I lacked. I focused less on what material things I have not inherited with my name and instead employed the courage and work ethic that I have toward contributing to a legacy I want it to bear.

ANALYSIS

In this very powerful essay, the candidate effectively shares a very personal story with the reader: a story of struggle, determination, and success. By recounting her personal history, the author clearly explains the service mission that drives her to pursue an HBS education.

This applicant has clearly been impacted by her family's legacy and its heritage. Juxtaposing small vignettes about herself, her mother, and her sisters, she skillfully weaves in the life lessons that she has learned along the way. This essay exudes conviction, and the author comes across as a person who does not take commitment or responsibility lightly. In the concluding sentence, the applicant expands the scope of her essay from her personal life to what she hopes to contribute to society. She introduces her big-picture vision, which connects the dotted line from her past to her future. The applicant's ability to connect her personal story to her vision as a service-minded leader and to relate it to the reader makes this essay a success.

David Zhang

One day in 1989, not long after my parents and I set foot in America, we stumbled upon a piece of furniture that would come to define our early years as immigrants. Lying limply on a street corner in our Brooklyn neighborhood was a three-legged coffee table. The previous owner had abandoned it—surely for its obvious handicap—but on that lucky day, the three-legged table got a second chance at life and became part of our home.

We were so poor back then that even crippled furniture helped. In China, my mom worked as a chemist and my dad designed theater lighting. They were both college-educated and successful in their jobs, but a stingy communist economy and an unforgiving currency exchange fought against them in moving to America. The transatlantic flight devoured all their savings and left them at JFK International with two ratty suitcases, a seven-year-old son, and the courage to start over.

There's a Chinese saying, "Tears fall downward," referring to the sacrifices parents make for their children. My parents made theirs so that I didn't have to grow up in a country where tanks were deployed against students whose horrible crime was pleading for democracy. My parents' sacrifice eventually paid off, and within ten years, they purchased their first house in America and saw their son off to Harvard. The latter accomplishment belongs more to them than to me: the act of parenting validated.

Nothing, however, seemed more unlikely when we first arrived. Constrained by their broken English, my parents took what jobs they could find. They were outrageously overworked and underpaid, but they never brought any bitterness home.

What they did bring home was the occasional piece of abandoned furniture. My dad repaired the three-legged coffee table, recreating a fourth leg with the same passion and ingenuity that had driven his former success in lighting design. His handiwork did the job. The table served us reliably for years. It gave us a place to gather at dinnertime, to talk about my day at school, to hear stories of our family history and of our relatives in China, to share our hopes and dreams. That one piece of furniture is endlessly entwined with memories of my childhood. Whenever I think back to the things my parents taught me—about courage, sacrifice, optimism, creativity, and hard work—our coffee table was always somewhere in the room.

ANALYSIS

When answering this essay question, many applicants choose stories in which they can display their maturity, their vision of life, and how they acquired both. This particular candidate uses a very powerful image, a three-legged table mended by his father, as a metaphor for his life. That crooked table also embodies the life lessons he learned from his parents. In order to maintain the readers' interest, this candidate adopts a storytelling tone. He structures his essay chronologically, starting with his parents' arrival in the United States and ending with a philosophical conclusion about how a single image is enough to remind him of both his roots and his direction in life.

From this response, the reader truly understands where the applicant comes from. Literally, he is the scion of a poor Chinese immigrant family. Figuratively, he comes from a background of hard work, diligence, and humility. Both aspects have shaped his unique personality, and the reader understands that this applicant's words and feelings are genuine. In subtly paying tribute to his parents, "tears fall downward," the candidate endears the reader with his humility. By choosing this particular anecdote, the applicant achieves two goals: he conveys a sense of authenticity, and he demonstrates a high level of self-awareness. By turning an imperfect table into the anchor in his life, the author demonstrates the strength of his resolve and gives the reader a glimpse of his essence. If this essay is a vehicle for applicants to shed light on their personality, mission accomplished.

John Schmit

Some insight in to my life can be drawn from this experience.

A group of a hundred-plus parents gathered in a large ballroom to discuss the challenges and fears they face raising their children. In an effort to make this experience more intimate they created a large circle that stretched the borders of the ballroom.

The common bond uniting these parents is that all of them have at least one child born with albinism, a genetic condition that gives not only a unique appearance and resulting social stigmas, but also, in many cases, legal blindness.

They spent some time discussing their challenges—their children's educational difficulties, challenges with athletics, interpersonal struggles, and the constant comments and stares both they and their children receive outside their homes.

Now I was to be their guest speaker. The speaker who would discuss his experiences growing up with albinism and address any questions or concerns they might have. So I stood in the middle of that circle, a circle comprised of parents worried that their children will always be outsiders in this world. Parents struggling to grasp the visually limited realities of their children, and what those limitations will mean in their children's lives.

And I discussed my life. Through stories of my struggles and accomplishments I explained to those parents what was possible. I explained how their children could play baseball or any other sport despite their visual disability—and they had to let them try. I did have to preface this with the disclaimer that their children might be relegated in game time to right field in the top of the ninth when their team is up by sixteen, but it was a comment that also resonated with some of the fully sighted fathers in the room.

Many of those parents came up to me after my discussion and wanted their children to meet me. I, somehow, had suddenly become a role model to these parents—a hero they wanted their children to meet.

The positive impact I had made me realize the tremendous value my leadership and perspective could have on people touched by albinism. That realization is why I pursued and was elected to the board of directors of this group—the National Organization for Albinism and Hypopigmentation. It is an opportunity for me to give back and help others successfully manage the many challenges of albinism.

ANALYSIS

This essay recounts a unique and compelling tale. From the beginning, we are immediately drawn into an unusual setting. Why is the writer attending this event? Compelled to find out, we read on. The essay is structured like a speech, peppered with figures of style. He himself only appears toward the middle of the story with an engaging, "Now I was to be their guest speaker." The readers are captivated as they wonder: what can a hundred-plus parents learn from an HBS applicant?

The question is resolved in the next paragraph: the applicant, affected by albinism, is about to share his childhood experiences with parents eager to learn. In the speech, the author says he spoke about his life, a life that served to inspire an entire community. The applicant sends a very powerful, service-oriented message that emphasizes the cross-generational attributes of leadership. And leadership is indeed what he demonstrated in this essay: he was able to show resilience growing up and is now a source of inspiration. He leaves the readers with many introspective questions: How can you be a leader in every single area of your life? How can you turn your challenges into victories?

Jaime Arreola

I wish the admissions committee had asked me: What else inside the applicant personality is valuable to know?

More than just a PepsiCo marketing manager from Mexico with an engineering background, strong quantitative skills, and a lot of extracurricular work on his path to appear as a distinguished candidate, I'm a man who enjoys life. My unique family, my diverse friends and my always unsatisfied appetite for enjoying life, are what move the man inside of me.

My family feeds my heart and soul. I'm the oldest of thirty-five grandsons, and that makes me want to be a role model and create a living example for my younger cousins. Every vacation, I go home to a weeklong agenda of daily family events. Everybody in the family, from my seventy-eight-year-old grandmother to the youngest cousin, participates in each event. That's the way I grew up and the kind of family I aspire to build.

I value my friends and consider them my biggest asset. They are close to me at joyous events like my birthday, just as they are at sad times like my grandfather's funeral. I enjoy their different backgrounds and lifestyles—one is a movie director, and another will be a priest next year. Their variety reflects on my experiences. I survived during hard financial times at Monterrey by fixing my wealthier friends' gardens and cooking them elegant dinners; but just as often with my other friends, I won street soccer tournaments and taught poor kids to read. My friends make me stronger and are part of my greatest memories.

I value my attitude toward challenges. I can find the calm in the middle of a crisis, even if it means confronting my inner fears. I found my way to calm everybody's panic in the emergency room when my aunt had a car accident last year, and I was brave enough to bungee-jump in Niagara Falls.

Finally, I value my capability of enjoying the "little things" of life. A morning jog is my most inspiring moment of the day. The smile of a little kid moves me inside, and I get pleasure from laughing and making people laugh. I love to enjoy every moment that makes me feel successful, either going back home and giving Mom a sample of a new product I just launched, or having seafood and a beer after a week of hard work.

This is who I am, and this is what I bring anywhere I go. I consider myself fortunate for these things and I am looking to pay back what I've been lucky to receive. I consider myself a good man, and it's how I aspire to raise my kids, teaching them to enjoy the "little things" of life.

ANALYSIS

This essay is about the "little, yet important things in life." The applicant takes advantage of the flexibility allowed by this open-ended essay question to write a lighthearted yet compelling, description of both his family life and the lessons he has drawn from being a family man. This story highlights the applicant's struggles and determination and shows that he has not lost his focus, nor has he lost sight of what truly matters to him.

Other Question

The candidate gives the reader a chance to understand his family-oriented motivations that distinguish him in the context of an otherwise career-focused application. That is exactly why this essay is so memorable. Though this response might be accused of "abuse of clichés" and happily-ever-after anecdotes, the candidate strikes an interesting balance between family stories and personal struggle stories, which makes the essay work. Overall, this applicant effectively alternates between anecdotes from his unique family situation and the lessons he drew from it, stressing the importance of family, friendship, and the strength he has acquired from them.

ANONYMOUS

"So what's this farming thing all about?"

On my last train ride from Tarragona to Barcelona to catch my flight home after a semester abroad in Spain, I resolved to return after graduation for a more authentic Spanish experience.

In the last few months of my senior year, I found World-Wide Opportunities on Organic Farms (WWOOF). For $20, WWOOF provided me with a list of sixty-some farms in Spain that had agreed to provide food and lodging in exchange for a hard day's work.

I had already bought my ticket to Barcelona before making final arrangements with the Masía de Ginero farm in Valderrobres. The decision to experience an agrarian lifestyle without electricity or running water was not popular among my family and friends, but I wanted to test myself, to leap headfirst into a situation for which I had no background and see if I could swim.

After three months at Masía de Ginero, I had done much more than swim. I became a part of the family and an asset to the farm, plowing acres of potato fields, harvesting olives, building a hot water system, and helping to demolish a three-hundred-year-old stone hacienda. I came to appreciate the need to conserve water and electricity, the value of teamwork, and the satisfaction of a hearty meal after a long, physical day in the sun. But beside the enormous personal impact the experience had on me, it also ended up shaping my career path.

On my first day as a field hand, along with other area farmers, I performed the annual community chore of demucking the *açequia*, the millennia-old irrigation system that delivers water from a nearby lake to dozens of farms in this notoriously parched area of the country. As I trudged through miles of irrigation channels, slinging sludge over my shoulder, I couldn't help but contemplate the fact that without this simple yet crucial piece of infrastructure, this community would likely never have flourished.

Understanding the transformative effects of public works projects was a poignant lesson that I took with me when I returned to Washington, D.C., to find full-time work. I decided that my niche in international development would be to address the daunting but tangible problems that developing countries face, like impassable roads, lack of access to water, and spotty electricity distribution.

I will always believe in the value of reaching beyond my comfort zone, for without significant challenges, I will never truly know my full potential.

ANALYSIS

This essay has a very catchy beginning and maintains an idealistic tone throughout. The readers observe the applicant as he goes through a formative experience working on a rustic organic farm in Spain. The overall story is well-structured and demonstrates that the candidate is introspective. The author is fantastically descriptive, explaining the rudimentary, simple conditions on the farm. The candidate also exemplifies commitment by following through on an unusual plan. In fact, this is the most salient point of the essay. The applicant shows vulnerability and the willingness to be touched by subjects that did not necessarily concern him directly. He showed his willingness to act and create change, qualities that would make him a fine addition to the Harvard Business School community.

Though the story is compelling, this essay could have been significantly strengthened had the author highlighted lessons he learned along the way. While offering conclusions are important, it is often the thought-process development behind those takeaways that offer the reader the most insight into an applicant's personality.

Ally Ip

I would like to share with the admissions board my lifelong passion in physical fitness, because it defines an important part of my personality. If accepted into HBS, I expect to be an active member of the school's athletic communities.

I am five-foot-two, which is very short by military standards. To lead effectively in a "macho" environment lik the U.S. Army, I have to demonstrate competency in the physical area. My devotion in martial arts gave me a head start. At MIT, I joined the Korean Karate Club about the same time I enrolled in the ROTC. In 1996, I represented the club in the Green Belt Division of the World Tae-Kwon-Do Association Northeast Regional Tournament, and won championships in both the form and the free-style matches. In the 1997 Brown Belt Division, I won both contests again. In the 1998 Black Belt Division, I lost the free-style match to a more experienced black belt, but continue to claim championship in the form category.

These awards gave me instant recognition among my bigger colleagues in the Army. In one of my Army sparring classes, my opponent was a boxer, and the spectators thought that I would be beaten in thirty seconds. In fact, it took me only fifteen seconds to win the fight. In 2002, I further proved my physical capability by earning first place in the Female Division Weight-Lifting competition of the 1-43 ADA Battalion Winter Olympics. My commander was astonished after the competition, "Ally, where in that tiny body do you hold that strength?" Bigger is not necessary better!

Also in 2002, I represented the U.S. Army Air Defense Artillery Branch in the Army 10-Miler, the nation's largest. Then, in 2003, I qualified for a gold badge in the German Proficiency Badge, and was later certified as a trainer. In 2005, I was a trainer for the 35th ADA BDE in the Manchu Foot March. These are considered very tough physical challenges even for the male soldiers.

Recently, I earned a black belt in Hapkido, and am now an assistant instructor at the Osan Air Base. I may have decided to leave the U.S. Army next year, but that does not mean an end to my passion for physical fitness. It is a large part of who I am, and something that I am very proud of.

ANALYSIS

This essay screams energy. The applicant's personality is clearly transmitted through her choice of words and her choice of actions. Although her accomplishments can sound like an ineffective laundry list, the candidate manages to paint herself as an action-oriented individual with a strong resolve. She is a leader who also depicts herself as a real champion.

The essay is made all the more powerful because the candidate picked an unconventional way to shine, which has carried through all aspects of her life. Each victory of hers was a triple victory: over the odds, over others, and over herself. She is obviously proud of her successes and builds enough momentum from the beginning of the story for the reader to want to know more about this extraordinary woman.

One caveat of this approach is that this essay fails to explore the bigger picture. A sentence or two explaining how the candidate intends to translate her achievements (mostly physical) and her victories (mostly over herself) into HBS, the business world, and life outside the army would have greatly strengthened this response.

Nevertheless, the reader cannot help but admire this candidate's determination. This is a classic example of an applicant who was able to convey passion through focus on a single achievement. It is important to note that the lack of passion can turn any accomplishment into a dull, soporific story, but any true accomplishment can be made stellar and memorable if passion is the backbone.

Anonymous

At the age of seven, I left my "kid days" of playing banker behind to open a lemonade stand on the front porch. Capitalizing on my parents' planned garage sale, I sold cold drinks and red licorice to the visiting bargain-hunters. As the years passed, my ventures evolved into neighborhood car washes and a business called Personalized Urban Puppy Sitters (PUPS).

More than a young entrepreneurial instinct, I attribute my actions to the set of values I was imbued with by my parents. They succeeded in teaching me the importance of work and the value of money. While my friends received flat allowances of $20 a week, my sister and I received none. When I begged for the latest gimmicky toy, my mother said, "Save up your money and buy it." Sure enough, after I had saved enough to purchase a Nintendo set in the fifth grade, I was overflowing with pride. Granted, my sister and I only had enough money for one game, but we played it with relish.

At the age of eleven, I became an avid babysitter, filling my nights, weekends, and even early mornings with child-care commitments. By the time I took off for my junior year in Spain, I had enough savings to cover my personal expenses for the entire year abroad. Churros tasted sweeter and movies were more enjoyable remembering the work that afforded those luxuries.

While taking full loads to complete two bachelor's degrees, I held down several part-time jobs to help support myself through college (working from fifteen to twenty-five hours per week). This, on top of holding multiple club leadership positions and squeezing in time at the gym or with friends, caused friends to question how I fit life into twenty-four-hour days. But work has never been an optional item for me. Though my parents never demanded it, they have taught me why it is indispensable, and it has made me a more independent and disciplined individual.

ANALYSIS

In the context of the other essay topics, it might be difficult to explain how the author of this essay became hardworking, independent, and disciplined. The subject matter is not exactly a defining experience in leadership development, nor does it easily qualify as one of the three greatest accomplishments. Nonetheless, it effectively illustrates the author's everyday work ethic, as well as its origins.

At first glance, stories about selling soda and babysitting might appear banal, but the author clearly explains how those experiences played a formative role in her personal development. While the other essays in her application most likely describe an accomplished young businesswoman, this one affords a glimpse of how she got there. In this sense, the essay rounds out the application and allows the admissions committee to get to know the author on a more personal level.

Anonymous

I enjoy never giving up, always thinking there's a way, and if there is not one, creating it. I enjoy walking through Central Park with Paige, my girlfriend of six years, and discovering new paths. I enjoy helping Ground Zero construction workers by cold-calling major insole distributors and organizing five hundred pairs of insoles to be donated to the Red Cross. I enjoy seeing that the elevator has not moved off my floor between the time I come home late and when I wake up early to go running the next morning.

I enjoy having close friends with not-so-close personalities, histories, goals, and lifestyles. I have friends who work at Lehman and Solomon, and another who works at her mother's Common Grounds coffee shop; I have friends who visit families on opposite sides of the Dead Sea but can still have peaceful conversations about U.S. foreign policy.

I enjoy never having a single regret, standing in the present and leaning toward the future. I enjoy making mistakes and realizing my first impression was wrong. The best manager I ever worked for initially struck me as a timid and uninspiring person. Weeks later I realized how her unthreatening nature was an incredibly powerful tool in putting clients at ease with changing their minds and with accepting her bold and innovative ideas.

I enjoy listening, learning, trying new things, and growing. I enjoy finally learning to surf Costa Rica's fifteen-foot waves after spending the better part of two days underwater. I enjoy seeing my first boss finally laugh when I built up the nerve to do an impression of her at the company Christmas party. I enjoy laughing, making people laugh, and people that can laugh at themselves.

I enjoy how my family's diversity has shaped me. My younger brother, who spent time in three different high schools, is beginning to act on my coaching that straightening up his act does not mean living an uninteresting life. While my father grew up playing stickball on the streets of Queens, New York, my mother learned how to sail her father's boat on Lake Lucerne in Switzerland. I enjoy my parents' different renditions of my childhood. I enjoy knowing that my personality lies, like the truth in their contrasting tales, somewhere in between.

ANALYSIS

As an essay intended to supplement a business school application with personal details, this effort is a tour de force. Every sentence conveys something new about the author—about his interests, feelings, hobbies, and cultural identity. His insatiable appetite for life is impossible to ignore. The seemingly endless list of details, when taken as a whole, paints a picture of a fascinating and complex individual. The essay is unassuming and unpretentious, while its honesty makes it instantly credible.

Much like the preceding example, the essay adds tremendous depth to the application. The driven banker becomes a candidate with a very broad and balanced view of the world, able to contribute to his MBA community not just a finance skill set, but a deep perspective on happy living.

Cabin Kim

Their dramatic peaks and graceful curves speak volumes.

Chinese characters are expressive, beautiful, deep. Chinese "words" are pictures of ideas, communicating a concept as both what it is and is not. For instance, the character for "man" joins a farmer's field with an arm of strength; to the Chinese, a male without vocation is not truly a man. My life is not just about who I am, but also who I am not. Back in high school, I was an accomplished cellist. Still, I harbored no illusions about music as a professon, and college life beckoned for my time. I am no longer that cellist; recently, as I played in a trio for a wedding, the violinist repeatedly winced at my good intentions.

Halfway through college, I found myself envying my roommate for his drawing class assignments—I was starving for creative expression. After tasting southern China during a summer Christian mission, I registered for a Chinese class. I was forewarned by Chinese friends who had taken Mandarin at Duke: they, from Chinese-language homes, could barely handle the workload . . . why should I, lacking Chinese background, risk my schedule or my transcript? But life encompasses not just what I choose, but also what I avoid. How could I retreat from the challenge of Chinese before the first day of class?

My three semesters of Chinese were a delight. For hours at a stretch, I hid in the library to write characters, millennia of culture and wisdom flowing through my hand.

I chose to embrace the beauty, expression, and depth of the Chinese language, and the fruit of my choice has become a part of me.

ANALYSIS

While several of the preceding essays present a breadth of experience, Cabin focuses on a single interest. The point, however, is not so much his diligent study of the Chinese language and calligraphy, but rather the philosophical question of choosing challenges in life. The anecdotes demonstrate Cabin's ability to decide which battles are simply not worth fighting. A sense of deep self-awareness permeates the text and implicitly attests to his maturity and poise.

It may seem that this essay has nothing to do with business at all, but Cabin's introspective skill is likely to be instrumental in his future decision-making in a corporate context. In a very subtle and elegant way, Cabin strengthens his image as a qualified future business leader.